2004

Poems and Prose from the Old English

TRANSLATED BY

BURTON RAFFEL

EDITED BY ALEXANDRA H. OLSEN

AND BURTON RAFFEL

INTRODUCTIONS BY

ALEXANDRA H. OLSEN

YALE UNIVERSITY PRESS

NEW HAVEN AND LONDON

Poems

and Prose

from the

Old English

Designed by Nancy Ovedovitz and set in Monotype Bembo
type by Tseng Information Systems, Inc. Printed in the United
States of America by Vail-Ballou Press, Binghamton, New York.

Library of Congress Cataloging-in-Publication Data
Poems from the Old English
Poems and prose from the Old English / translated by Burton
Raffel ; edited by Alexandra H. Olsen and Burton Raffel ;
introductions by Alexandra H. Olsen.
p. cm.
ISBN 0-300-06994-4 (cloth : alk. paper). — ISBN
0-300-06995-2 (pbk. : alk. paper)
1. English literature—Old English, ca. 450–1100—Modernized
versions.   2. Civilization, Anglo-Saxon—Literary collections.
3. Civilization, Medieval—Literary collections.   4. Anglo-
Saxons—Literary collections.   I. Raffel, Burton.   II. Olsen,
Alexandra Hennessey.   III. Title.
PR1508.P59   1998
829′.08—dc21   97-22556

A catalogue record for this book is available from the British
Library.

The paper in this book meets the guidelines for permanence
and durability of the Committee on Production Guidelines for
Book Longevity of the Council on Library Resources.

10 9 8 7 6 5 4 3 2 1

a.h.o.: to Gary L. Olsen, *uncer giedd geador*

b.r.: to the memory of Morton Bloomfield, with whom I first studied Old English

Contents

Introduction

The Anglo-Saxon or Old English period dates from A.D. 449 to 1066. The first date is shrouded in legendary history. According to the *Anglo-Saxon Chronicle,* the Romano-British king Vortigern hired troops from the Continent to help him in his wars against the Picts, the ancient inhabitants of north and central Scotland, following the Roman troop withdrawal from Britain. Shortly thereafter, the Germanic warriors who came to England at Vortigern's invitation asked warriors from three Germanic tribes, the Angles, the Saxons, and the Jutes, to come to Britain. The tribes, under the leadership of two brothers, Horsa and Hengest (which means "Stallion"), came and seized the land from the Britons, the inhabitants of present-day England. The second date, 1066, is clearly historical. On September 28, 1066, William, duke of Normandy, landed an army at Pevensey and on October 14 encountered the English defenders at the Battle of Hastings. Just as the arrival of the Anglo-Saxons in 449 had tremendous consequences for the island of Britain, so did the Norman Conquest: the period of the Anglo-Saxons' dominance of language, laws, and customs had ended.

Widespread settlement followed the Anglo-Saxons' arrival in 449. They came in scattered groups, so there was no central authority, and each area had a local ruler. The numbers and boundaries of these petty "tribal" kingdoms shifted with the fortunes of war. Generally speaking, three kingdoms in the north and northeast were settled by people who called themselves "Angles": Northumbria, from the Humber River to the Firth of Forth; Mercia, from the Humber to the Wash and inland toward the Bristol Channel; and East Anglia, occupying the hump of land south of the Wash. The Isle of Wight and Britain's southeastern tip, which became the kingdom of Kent, were settled by "Jutes." "Saxons" settled in Essex, between East Anglia and Kent, Sussex on the southern coast to the west of Kent, and Wessex, bounded by Cornwall, the Bristol Channel, and the English Channel.

The Anglo-Saxon tribes who came to Britain were similar to other Germanic tribes. Their society was of the kind called "heroic," organized for war, with a code of values that emphasized physical and moral courage. The most important bond was therefore that between the lord and his retainers, who formed a warband we call the *comitatus,* meaning "retinue or following." The lord was obligated to protect and reward his men. The poetry of this society is filled with images of the lord who gives gifts and receives love and loyalty. In return, the men defend him, swearing that if he dies in battle they will not retreat behind the place where he fell and will die if they must. Their relationship is described most vividly in the tenth-century poem *The Battle of Maldon:* "Our minds must be stronger, our hearts / Braver, our courage higher, as our numbers / Shrink" (312–314).

The comitatus was composed of young, single men tightly knit in what the Germans call the *Männerbund,* "bond of men." Marriage took older men out of the comitatus, though they continued to fight in war. Marriage and the comitatus were voluntary associations. By contrast, the family unit, the organizing unit of society, was involuntary, and one's obligations to the family were a matter of duty. Judging from the literary and historical record, women held high status in Anglo-Saxon society: women were respected for their wise counsel and played important roles in all classes. Aristocratic women in both literature and history were assertive in speech, which was as important as action in Germanic society. At the bottom of the social scale were serfs, who performed the agricultural labor necessary for the survival of this premodern society. The extant texts are primarily those of the elite class; only occasionally is there a reference to a member of the lower class, such as the swineherd who avenged the ealdorman Cumbran in the narrative in the *Anglo-Saxon Chronicle* for 755 or the Frisian sailor's wife in *Maxims I.*

The tribes stressed the importance of courage, personal honor, loyalty, and kin. The bond between a man and his sister's son was particularly strong, for reasons that predate the written record. The rules and institutions of society were preserved not by a public system of justice but by a private system, the blood feud. In this system, if a member of a family was killed, someone from that family killed the slayer or a member of his family in revenge. Blood feuds are a common theme in Old English poetry. As time passed, the blood feud was mitigated by a system of payment called the *wergeld,* or "man-price." This was a system of fines graduated according to the extent of the injury and the rank of the person killed or injured. There was, however, no wergeld for a king, as the *Chronicle* passage for 755 clearly dramatizes. King Cynewulf's men swear "that none of their kinsmen was dearer to them than their lord, and they would never serve and follow the man who killed him." They kill their kinsmen to avenge their dead lord.

Anglo-Saxon society seems to have been basically homogeneous, and as far as can be gleaned from the scanty records, all classes shared common assumptions about the nature of human life. The worst misery was exile, separation from the community. We see the grief of exile in *The Wanderer* and *A Woman's Lament.* The Wanderer "follows . . . the sea, sailing endlessly, / Aimlessly, in exile" (4–5), while the woman lives apart from the community "in an earthen cavern under an oak" (28). (In Norse literature, which provides information that helps explicate Old English, oaks are associated with disgrace and execution, raising the possibility that the woman may be in the ultimate exile of death.) In *The Seafarer,* exile is chosen voluntarily as a pilgrimage on the sea. The Seafarer says, "And yet my heart wanders away, / My soul roams with the sea" (58–59) because "the kingdoms of earth" (81) are transient.

The Anglo-Saxons had a strong sense of *wyrd,* "what will be, fate," which they believed governed the lives of human beings and the course of worldly events. "Fate blows hardest on a bleeding heart" (59), observes the Wanderer. He adds, "Man is fleeting, woman is fleeting" (109): the Old English word for "fleeting" is *læne,* "lent."

Everything in life is a loan; human beings own nothing themselves. People who accepted their destiny with dignity and courage could achieve a good name and fame that outlived them. The last word of *Beowulf* is *lofgeornost,* "most eager for praise," and that word can sum up the desires of both historical and literary heroes.

During the ninth century, the royal house of Wessex established an overlordship of England, partly in response to the need for a united effort against a new wave of Viking invaders from Scandinavia. The invasions had begun in 794, during the reign of King Beorhtic (reigned 786–802), when Wessex was attacked by three *scipu Deniscra monna,* "ships of Danish men," precursors of the series of Viking invasions in the ninth century. As the invasions increased in ensuing decades, the Wessex king Ethelred (reigned 865–871), assisted by his brother Alfred, struggled against a great Viking army that was led by the sons of the famous Viking Ragnarr Loðbrók. Alfred continued to fight the invaders after succeeding to the throne on his brother's death in 871, according to the established practice of lateral succession. In 878, Alfred defeated the Danes decisively at Edington, after which the Danish king Guthrum and thirty others were baptized, and in 879 the Viking army disbanded, although the Vikings had made permanent settlements in Northumbria, Mercia, and East Anglia. Alfred the Great took advantage of the peace to reorganize the national defense and build a system of fortresses. Among Alfred the Great's other achievements were the revival of learning and the establishment of a strong, centralized monarchy.

Alfred was succeeded by his son, Edward the Elder, initiating the custom of primogeniture. Edward and his sister, Ethelfleda, who was also the wife of Ethelred of Mercia, brought Alfred's defense fortifications to completion. As "lord of the Mercians" (*hlaford Myrcena*), Ethelred had been Alfred's subordinate, and Ethelfleda therefore was known as *hlæfdige Myrcena,* "lady of the Mercians." Ethelfleda took over the rule of Mercia during her husband's illness, before his death in 911, and ruled it until her own death in 918. The fragmentary version of the *Anglo-Saxon Chronicle* known as the *Mercian Register* surveys her activities in collaboration with her brother, building fortresses and fighting against both the Welsh and the Vikings. Ethelfleda's career demonstrates the importance of the dynasty of Alfred and helps define the role of women in Anglo-Saxon England.

The fifth-century Anglo-Saxons were largely unlettered, even though they had a runic alphabet that they used for inscriptions. There are indications that they had a system of orally composed poetry comparable to that among the ancient Greeks, the Xhosa of South Africa, and the peoples of the former Yugoslavia. Extrapolating from the extant poetry of other Germanic tribes, references to such poetry in Latin works, and the small amount of Anglo-Saxon poetry that has survived in late manuscripts (c. 1000), these songs were very probably narrative or eulogistic, evoking the values of a warrior community and concerning historical material of importance to that community. Many scholars assume that *Beowulf,* the oldest English epic, is an oral-derived work. *Beowulf* tells the story of the battles of the hero Beowulf against the troll-like Grendel and Grendel's mother and against a fire-breathing dragon. It is several generations removed from the original composition. Nevertheless, it provides some hints about the nature of fifth-century society and the poetry that may have been composed at that time.* Although composed in England, it is set on the Continent, and the references to historical figures attest to the historicity of the original. The surviving poetry includes the fragmentary *Battle of Finnsburh,* which tells a story parallel to the Finn digression of *Beowulf.* Some surviving poems are short works — elegies, riddles, and maxims — that could have been passed down relatively unchanged by memorial tradition.

Poetry was composed by a *scop,* a term with an uncertain etymology but which means a poet or singer, presumably originally oral, because the term seems to derive from preliterate days. Based on the information in such late Latin sources as Priscus's *History of the Goths* (A.D. 448), we can deduce that the fifth-century Germanic tribes (including the Anglo-Saxons) had professional singers who accompanied themselves on the harp. These professional singers

---

*The date and method of composition of *Beowulf* are matters of conjecture; I am adopting the views of John Miles Foley in "*Beowulf* and the Old English Poetic Tradition," *Immanent Art: From Structure to Meaning in Traditional Oral Epic* (Bloomington: Indiana University Press, 1991), 190–242.

were tribal historians, entertainers, and teachers; they also composed satirical verses. Old English literature provides some information about the scop. In *Beowulf,* when the Danes return from following the water-monster Grendel's tracks the morning after Beowulf and Grendel have fought, the poet includes a passage about a scop composing a poem in praise of Beowulf. The English monk Bede's *Ecclesiastical History of the English People,* an important Latin source for history of the period 597–731, states that people composed verses at banquets, accompanied by a harp. The poetry the herdsman Caedmon (fl. 670) composed for the angel who came to him in a vision, however, lacked musical accompaniment. Old English poetry was presumably presented orally (although the extant texts may not have been orally composed), with a lyre or harp providing a rhythmic beat.

However the poetry was composed, it uses an additive style, formulaic diction, and themes. The building blocks of a traditional narrative are termed *formulas,* abstract verbal patterns whose metrical and syntactical contours are fixed but whose actual words vary depending on the alliterative context. A famous example comes from *Beowulf,* "X spoke, son of Y." The formulas are units larger than a single word available to the author in constructing his narrative. *Themes* are recurrent scenic units, such as Exile, the Beasts of Battle (the wolf, the raven, and the sea-eagle who accompany armies), and the Hero on the Beach (the hero at the beginning or end of a journey in a situation between territories).

Literacy in the modern sense of the term came to Anglo-Saxon England in 597. Although Roman Britain had been Christian, Christianity became a minority religion during the Anglo-Saxon conquest. A mission sent by Pope Gregory the Great in 597, headed by the monk Augustine of Canterbury, converted the kingdom of Kent. From there, Christianity gradually spread throughout England, first to Northumbria when the Kentish princess Ethelbeorg married the pagan king Edwin. She was accompanied by her chaplain, the bishop Paulinus, who converted the king and his kingdom. In the same period, Irish missionaries made converts in the north of England. The Roman Catholic and Irish churches had different customs and styles of church governance, but in 664, the Synod of Whitby (presided over by the abbess Hild) decided that the English church should follow Roman rather than Celtic practices. In addition to Christian ideas, the missionaries introduced the Roman alphabet and the custom of writing.

Literacy was originally the possession of the clerical classes, and Latin was the language of scholarship. There were important schools at Canterbury and York, as well as at monasteries like Jarrow, where English was also taught. From the eighth century on, we can speak of a literate culture parallel to the unlettered majority's oral culture. Among the most valuable of monastic contributions was the systematic copying of Latin and English manuscripts. The Latin epistles known collectively as *The Boniface Collection* (c. 716–786) are in part the work of Saint Boniface, apostle of Germany, and his coworkers. The collection includes letters between men and women devoted to a common missionary goal. The missionaries on the Continent write to request manuscripts, and the monks and nuns in England speak of the works they have sent or been unable to send. The laments about *exulem Germanicum,* or "exile among the Germans," of Boniface remind a reader of the theme of exile in Old English poetry.

The world of Latin literacy is typified by Aldhelm (died 709), a West-Saxon of great learning, and the Venerable Bede (673?–735). Neither man, of course, wrote in the vernacular, but in Latin. Aldhelm wrote a great deal, including *De Virginitate,* "On Virginity," for the nuns of Barking Abbey. Bede was an oblate (that is, he had not yet taken monastic vows) at the Benedictine monastery of Jarrow in childhood and did not travel widely as an adult. Along with his comprehensive *Ecclesiastical History,* he wrote numerous works on metrics, astronomy, hagiography, meteorology, and medicine. Bede's Latin is expert and elegant, and his encyclopedic learning exemplifies that of the eighth-century literate class. This learned movement, which was primarily localized in the north of England, is called the Northumbrian Renaissance.

The Anglo-Saxons were leaders in scholarship, literature, and art during this period. Another famous Englishman of the time, some of whose works are extant, was Alcuin (died 804), who ran the emperor Charlemagne's palace school at Aachen in Germany. In addition to literature and illuminated manuscripts, Anglo-Saxon England produced all manner of expertly crafted weapons, utensils, decorative objects, and such household items as hinges, purses, locks, keys, and the like. The most noteworthy archaeological find to date is the royal ship burial at Sutton Hoo, discovered in 1939 and excavated by Charles W. Phillips, which includes jewelry, bowls, and coins.

After the Viking invasions, many monastic libraries were destroyed, especially in Northumbria, and people therefore had diminished access to written texts. King Alfred the Great ordered translated into English those works he deemed "needful that all men know." Alfred himself did some of the translations. Because of the loss of Latin learning, he wanted to train people to read at least their native language. Alfred initiated an age of vernacular literacy, a second flowering of civilization, centered at Winchester. One of the works translated into English was Bede's *Ecclesiastical History of the English People*. Alfred's belief in the importance of vernacular literature is also shown by the *Anglo-Saxon Chronicle*. The monks at Winchester began to systematize the annals and add annually accounts of important events so that all monasteries might have a shared history. The *Peterborough Chronicle* continued to be written in Old English until 1155, after which it is possible to declare that England had decisively reached the Middle English period.

One famous story recounted in the *Ecclesiastical History* is that of the poet Caedmon, reputed to have been the first person to compose Christian Old English poetry. According to Bede, Caedmon was an unlettered cowherd who regularly left the banquet table when the harp drew near and he was about to be required to sing. One night, he received a miraculous gift: an angel brought him the gift of song, and he composed a short work known as *Caedmon's Hymn*. A number of manuscripts of the Old English version of the *Ecclesiastical History* contain the Old English poem, one of the earliest datable works written down before the Norman Conquest. This history tells us that Caedmon's "poetry and singing were so delightful to hear that the very men who had taught him wrote down what came from his mouth and studied it"—a description of the means by which oral poetry is thought to have come into writing.

Most of the extant Old English poetry, like most medieval poetry, is anonymous. The identification of particular poems with particular poets represents a distinctive later change. However, works by three Old English poets have survived. Bede and Caedmon are represented by one poem each. Cynewulf, about whom nothing is known, is represented by four poems. Like Bede, Aldhelm is supposed to have composed vernacular poetry, but none has survived. The English monk and historian William of Malmesbury (1090?–1143?), however, reports that King Alfred's *Handboc,* "Handbook" (not extant), says that Aldhelm was without peer as an English poet.

When vernacular literacy flourished, works of many different kinds—both literary and nonliterary—were recorded. This includes Old English poetry. Four extant manuscripts (all c. 1000) include poetry: *The Exeter Book* (an anthology of Old English poems), *The Junius Manuscript, The Vercelli Book,* and *MS Cotton Vitellius A.x,* which includes *Beowulf.* In *MS Cotton Vitellius A.x,* in one of the hands in which *Beowulf* is written, is also found *Judith,* a retelling of an Old Testament book in heroic form. The other long poems, *Elene, Juliana, Andreas,** and *The Fates of the Apostles,* are all hagiographic, narrating the exploits not of a hero like Beowulf but of Christian saints. It is noteworthy that two of the hagiographic poems and *Judith* depict a woman as hero. *Elene* and *Juliana* use formulas and themes much as *Beowulf* does; these would have helped an oral scop develop his poem and presumably served a similar function for a literate poet composing in an oral-derived style. Both *Elene* and *Juliana* also include epilogues in which the poet requests prayers and weaves his name ("Cynewulf") in runes into his text.

The centuries that separate the Anglo-Saxon period from the modern world mean that manuscripts have survived from the period only by chance. Often the survival of a particular document or literary work must be ascribed not to its intrinsic merit but to its (and our) good fortune. The Old English manuscript containing *The Battle of Maldon,* for example, was almost completely destroyed in a fire in 1731, and the leaves including *Maldon* were completely lost. But a copy had been made in 1724 by a librarian, and all subsequent editions are directly or indirectly based on this transcription. The only source of *The Battle of Finnsburh* is a version printed by George Hickes in the eighteenth century. Hickes says that he found the fragmentary poem on one leaf in a volume of homilies (that is, sermons) in the library of Lambeth Palace, but the leaf has been lost

---

*The language of *Andreas* is so similar to that of *Beowulf* that scholars suspect an interdependence between the two poems.

again. In the case of both *Maldon* and *Finnsburh,* a scholar cannot
check the accuracy of the transcription or apply modern paleographi-
cal techniques to the manuscripts.

In all civilizations, poetry precedes prose. The eighth and ninth
centuries show the beginnings of extended prose in Old English,
principally though not exclusively homilies, as well as legal docu-
ments like wills. These wills were known by many terms, especially
gewrit, "writing," but also *cwide,* "speech or discourse," which attests to
their oral origin. The ealdorman Ethelwold ends his will by asserting
that the act of speech was paramount: *swaswa ic nu þam freondon sæde
þæ ic to spræc,* "exactly as I have informed my friends that it should
be." The extant wills list the gifts of the testator, both of land and of
property, to lay and ecclesiastical recipients. They demonstrate the
beginning of testamentary power, though the claims of tradition and
of lord and kin remain strong. The will of King Alfred the Great, in
particular, contains a wealth of historical information, and the one
bequest Alfred mentions, other than lands and money, is his sword,
a detail reminiscent of *Beowulf.* His laws show a wise and concerned
legislator, and his treaty with the King Guthrum of Denmark is a
model document. As we have noted, Alfred's educational program
produced translations of great Latin works by Bede, Gregory the
Great, and Augustine.

By the tenth century, Anglo-Saxon learning was recovering from
the Viking invasions. The tenth century is the age of a religious
and educational movement known as the Benedictine Reform, a
period of monastic reform that emphasized the importance of the
Benedictine rule and of learning and scholarship. The most important
literary figure of this reform is Aelfric, known as the Grammarian
(c. 955–1012). His writing is sensitive and imaginative, and his work
is marked by its pedagogical purpose. Aelfric wrote many pedagogical
works, including the first Latin grammar in a European vernacular
and a work known as the *Glossary,* a Latin-English dictionary of
several hundred words. Part of Aelfric's educational program involved
the composition and compilation of homilies arranged according
to the liturgical year. Like King Alfred, he used the vernacular as a
vehicle to discuss religious doctrine. He was concerned to help the
clergy, then suffering from the effects of the Viking attacks, to under-

stand the major tenets of Christianity and the sweep of Christian history from Creation to the Last Judgment. Aelfric argues that the Church on earth participates in the eternal order of God's kingdom. Another of his pedagogical works is the *Dialogues,* whose Latin title is the *Colloquium,* or "Colloquy," a model conversation between a teacher and his students.

Another prominent figure of this period is Wulfstan (died 1023), who became bishop of London in 996 and archbishop of York in 1002. In addition to his homilies, Wulfstan was a political theorist and jurist and drafted the laws of King Cnut. His sermons are concerned with eschatology and the "last things" (death, judgment, and heaven and hell). The *Sermo Lupi ad Anglos,* "Sermon of the Wolf to the English," is his most famous work. Written during a period of defeat by the Danes, the *Sermo* surveys the state of affairs in England and interprets it as God's judgment on a sinful society.

By the tenth century, literacy was apparently becoming more widespread, judging from the anonymous tenth-century *Blickling Homilies,* which were written for a popular audience. The ninth and tenth centuries were also the beginning of literate ways of thinking and doing business, when legal matters are recorded in writing and in English. More than 1,600 charters granting land survive, and there are also marriage agreements and manumissions of slaves. The wills of people other than a king like Alfred show us the goods owned by members of the nobility, men and women like those celebrated in the extant poetry. It is noteworthy that 40 percent of the extant wills are by women, a fact that tells us much about the position of women in Anglo-Saxon society. The situation changed after the Norman Conquest, because government, the legal system, and the ecclesiastical hierarchy were the provinces of those who spoke Norman French. English became once more an oral language, spoken primarily by the disempowered. When it emerged once more as a literary language, c. 1250, both it and the literature written in therein had changed dramatically.

The purpose of this volume is to introduce the Anglo-Saxons in words nuanced and supple enough to convey a sense of the original poetry and prose. In addition, as Robert P. Creed said in the Foreword to the first edition of *Poems from the Old English,* "The translations which appear in this volume are *poems*. They are in varying degrees and in various ways faithful to the letter of the Old English. . . . These poems can and will be read and judged for themselves, for the precise shapes they give to sound, for the fine excitement of their rhythm." They have been widely read (and reprinted) since their first appearance in book form, in 1960. It is our hope that, in this revised, restructured, and much enlarged volume, they (and the prose translations newly added) will continue to be both useful and enjoyable.

A Note to the Reader: Words followed by a bullet—as, for example, mead-hall• pleasures—are explained in the Glossary.

Selected Bibliography

TRANSLATIONS

Bede. *A History of the English Church and People.* Translated by Leo Sherley-Price. Harmondsworth: Penguin, 1955.

Garmonsway, George N. *The Anglo-Saxon Chronicle.* London: Everyman, 1953.

Nicholson, Lewis E., trans. *The Vercelli Book Homilies: Translations from the Anglo-Saxon.* Lanham, Md.: University Press of America, 1991.

Raffel, Burton. *Beowulf.* New York: New American Library, 1963.

Swanton, Michael James, trans. *Anglo-Saxon Prose.* London: Dent, 1975.

Whitelock, Dorothy, ed. *English Historical Documents.* Vol. 1, *c. 55–1042.* London: Oxford University Press, 1955.

HISTORY AND BACKGROUND

Bruce-Mitford, Rupert. *The Sutton Hoo Ship Burial,* 3 vols. London: British Museum, 1975, 1978, 1983.

Fell, Christine. *Women in Anglo-Saxon England.* Oxford: Basil Blackwell, 1986.

Hill, David. *An Atlas of Anglo-Saxon England, 700–1066.* Oxford: Basil Blackwell, 1981.

Hunter-Blair, Peter. *An Introduction to Anglo-Saxon England,* 2d ed. Cambridge: Cambridge University Press, 1977.

————. *The World of Bede.* London: Secker and Warburg, 1970.

Stenton, Doris Mary. *The English Woman in History.* London: Allen and Unwin, 1957.

Stenton, Frank M. *Anglo-Saxon England.* Oxford: Clarendon Press, 1943.

Whitelock, Dorothy. *The Beginnings of English Society.* Harmondsworth: Penguin, 1952.

LITERARY CRITICISM

Damico, Helen. *Beowulf's Wealhtheow and the Valkyrie Tradition.* Madison: University of Wisconsin Press, 1984.

Damico, Helen, and Alexandra H. Olsen. *New Readings on Women in Old English Literature.* Bloomington: Indiana University Press, 1990.

Green, Martin. *The Old English Elegies: New Essays in Criticism and Research.* Rutherford, N.J.: Fairleigh Dickinson University Press, 1983.

Greenfield, Stanley B., and Daniel G. Calder. *A New Critical History of Old English Literature.* New York: New York University Press, 1986.

O'Keefe, Katherine O'Brien. *Visible Song: Transitional Literacy in Old English Verse.* Cambridge Studies in Anglo-Saxon England, vol. 4. Cambridge: Cambridge University Press, 1990.

Renoir, Alain. *A Key to Old Poems: The Oral-Formulaic Approach to the Interpretation of West-Germanic Verse.* University Park: Pennsylvania State University Press, 1988.

Stevens, Martin, and Jerome Mandel. *Old English Literature: Twenty-Two Analytical Essays.* Lincoln: University of Nebraska Press, 1968.

PARALLEL WORKS

Old English literature is part of a larger European movement. Its poetry is related to the poetry of other Germanic peoples, and the prose is influenced by learned Latin continental culture. Therefore, the best reading context for the prose is provided by Latin works. Two recommended books are the following:

Albertson, Clinton, S.J. *Anglo-Saxon Saints and Heroes.* New York: Fordham University Press, 1967. [Latin lives of saints, narrated to present them as the heroes of the new religion.]

Talbot, C. H. *The Anglo-Saxon Missionaries in Germany.* New York: Sheed and Ward, 1954. [Lives of the members of the Boniface mission, including some of the correspondence of Saint Boniface.]

The best reading context for the poetry is the poetry of other Germanic societies, some of which is probably later than Beowulf.

Dickins, Bruce. *Runic and Heroic Poems of the Old Teutonic Peoples.* Cambridge: Cambridge University Press, 1915. [This volume includes *The Hildebrandslied,* a fragment, copied on the flyleaves of a volume of Latin homilies, of an Old High German poem about a battle between a father and son.]

Kratz, Dennis M., ed. and trans. *Waltharius and Ruodlieb.* Garland Library of Medieval Literature, vol. 13, ser. A. New York: Garland, 1984. [The *Poem of Walter* was written in Latin, possibly in the ninth century at Saint Gall, Switzerland. The poem has Germanic, Classical, and Christian elements and is of special interest for its depiction of the hostageship of Walter and Hildegund at the court of Attila, king of the Huns.]

Terry, Patricia. *Poems of the Elder Edda,* rev. ed. Philadelphia: University of Pennsylvania Press, 1990. [Poems that narrate the traditional Scandinavian stories of gods and heroes (male and female) in oblique and allusive language. Their emphasis on *góðan getr,* "good fame," recalls that of Old English poetry.]

A reading context for Christian poetry is the following:

Allen, Michael J. B., and Daniel G. Calder, trans. *Sources and Analogues of Old English Poetry: The Major Latin Texts in Translation.* Cambridge: D. S. Brewer, 1976.

TRANSLATION

Raffel, Burton. *The Art of Translating Poetry.* University Park: Pennsylvania State University Press, 1988.
———. *The Art of Translating Prose.* University Park: Pennsylvania State University Press, 1994.
———. *The Forked Tongue: A Study of the Translation Process.* The Hague: Mouton, 1971.

Poetry

Prosody and Style

Old English poetry is composed in lines that vary from seven to fourteen syllables. Each half-line normally has two stressed syllables, and two or three of the four stresses — never all four — alliterate.* In some poems an extra foot• is added to a normal half-line, producing a line that is called "hypermetric." In the first half-line, the extra stressed syllable participates in the alliteration• of the line, but in the second, it does not always do so. Hypermetric lines tend to occur in groups, often for no apparent reason, though sometimes for narrative importance. Hypermetric lines are here indicated first by a virgule (/) after the first half-line and then by dropping down and beginning the second half-line at the point where the first ends. In this way, the half-lines are both typographically and prosodically distinct.

Old English poetry is characterized by the use of parallelism•

---

*As noted of *Elene,* line 22, sometimes a two-stress half-line seems to take the place of a full line. Raymond P. Tripp, Jr., notes that "the assumed omission" of *Beowulf* line 2792b need not be rectified (*More About the Fight with the Dragon* [New York: University Press of America, 1983], 234). Robert Payson Creed argues that "a verse line is a sequence of measures based on alliteration" (*Reconstructing the Rhythm of* Beowulf [Columbia: University of Missouri Press, 1990], 206), freeing us to accept manuscript readings.

and long sentences that are not periodic•. The diction uses many synonyms, so that God is referred to as *Scyppend,* "Shaper or Creator," *Weard,* "Guardian," *Drihten,* "Lord," and *Frea,* "Lord." The poetry uses few similes but many metaphors called "kennings•" by modern scholars.

Elegies

The brief poems known as elegies are lyrics (that is, songs) that form a group similar in theme and tone. The speaker (whether the author or a fictional persona) sings of loss, grief, and, above all, exile. Each of the seven poems suggests but does not narrate a story.

The two most famous (and most frequently translated and anthologized) elegies are *The Wanderer* and *The Seafarer*. In *The Wanderer,* the loss lamented is that of a lord, because of which the speaker is in exile. He says movingly, "I've drunk too many lonely dawns, / Gray with mourning" (8–9), and turns to God for consolation:

> It's good to find your grace
> In God, the heavenly rock/
> where rests our every hope.
>
> (114–115)

The Wanderer contrasts the cold and friendlessness of the sea to the warmth and fellowship of land in the company of a generous lord and a comitatus. *The Seafarer* acknowledges the same opposition:

> Who could understand,
> In ignorant ease, what we others suffer
> As the paths of exile stretch endlessly on?
>
> (55–57)

However, this speaker chooses to go on sea voyages, and his "soul roams with the sea" (59). Most critics believe that he has chosen voluntary exile from society in order to save his soul:

> Thus the joys of God
> Are fervent with life, where life itself
> Fades quickly into the earth.
>
> (64–66)

Several of the elegies lament the loss, not of a lord, but of a loved one. *A Woman's Lament* begins:

> This song of journeys into sorrow
> Is mine. I sing it. I alone
> Can ravel out its misery, full-grown
> When I was, and never worse than now.
>
> (1–4)

A Woman's Lament is spoken by a woman. (Old English was a language that had grammatical gender, and the endings used in *A Woman's Lament* [*geomorre*, "mournful," and *minre sylfre*, "my own self"] indicate that the speaker is female.) She voices her plight in the same type of language used by the Wanderer and the Seafarer, speaking of "the darkness of exile" (5). *Wulf and Eadwacer* is also spoken by a woman. It is so allusive that scholars cannot determine whether the woman is mourning the loss of a lover or a son, but in either case her grief and isolation are unmistakable. Raffel has translated the poem to make it express grief for the loss of a lover.

Two elegies spoken in a man's voice have different focuses from those of *The Wanderer* and *The Seafarer*. The speaker of *The Husband's Message* is a rune-stick carved by a man in exile and sent to his wife. In the background is the comitatus• relationship and the pleasures of the mead-hall•, but in the foreground is the man's exile from his wife:

> there's nothing more he wants,
> Oh prince's daughter, no precious gems,
> No stallions, no mead-hall• pleasure, no treasure
> On earth, but you.
>
> (44–47)

Deor, with its refrain "That passed, and so may this" (7), deals explic-
itly with exile and suffering, comparing Deor's plight to that of
legendary heroes. The name of the speaker, "Deor," which we learn in
line 37, means a wild beast and therefore an exile. He laments the loss
of his rank in society in terms analogous to the Wanderer's loss of his
lord.

Somewhat different is the seventh elegy, the fragmentary *The Ruin,*
which begins:

Fate has smashed these wonderful walls,
This broken city, has crumbled the work
Of giants.

(1–3)

The Ruin mourns, not the loss of a lord or a lover, but the monuments
of the past fallen into decay, the transience of everything made by
human beings.

THE WANDERER

This lonely traveler longs for grace,
For the mercy of God; grief hangs on
His heart and follows the frost-cold foam
He cuts in the sea, sailing endlessly,
Aimlessly, in exile. Fate has opened   5
A single port: memory. He sees
His kinsmen slaughtered again, and cries:
      "I've drunk too many lonely dawns,
Gray with mourning. Once there were men
To whom my heart could hurry, hot   10
With open longing. They're long since dead.
My heart has closed on itself, quietly
Learning that silence is noble and sorrow
Nothing that speech can cure. Sadness
Has never driven sadness off;   15
Fate blows hardest on a bleeding heart.
So those who thirst for glory smother
Secret weakness and longing, neither
Weep nor sigh nor listen to the sickness

In their souls. So I, lost and homeless,   20
Forced to flee the darkness that fell
On the earth and my lord.
                              Leaving everything,
Weary with winter I wandered out
On the frozen waves, hoping to find   25
A place, a people, a lord to replace
My lost ones. No one knew me, now,
No one offered comfort, allowed
Me feasting or joy. How cruel a journey
I've traveled, sharing my bread with sorrow   30
Alone, an exile in every land,
Could only be told by telling my footsteps.
For who can hear: 'friendless and poor,'
And know what I've known since the long cheerful nights
When, young and yearning, with my lord I yet feasted   35
Most welcome of all. That warmth is dead.
He only knows who needs his lord
As I do, eager for long-missing aid;
He only knows who never sleeps
Without the deepest dreams of longing.   40
Sometimes it seems I see my lord,
Kiss and embrace him, bend my hands
And head to his knee, kneeling as though
He still sat enthroned, ruling his thanes•.
And I open my eyes, embracing the air,   45
And see the brown sea-billows heave,
See the sea birds bathe, spreading
Their white-feathered wings, watch the frost
And the hail and the snow. And heavy in heart
I long for my lord, alone and unloved.   50
Sometimes it seems I see my kin
And greet them gladly, give them welcome,
The best of friends. They fade away,
Swimming soundlessly out of sight,
Leaving nothing.   55
                    How loathsome become
The frozen waves to a weary heart.

In this brief world I cannot wonder
That my mind is set on melancholy,
Because I never forget the fate   60
Of men, robbed of their riches, suddenly
Looted by death—the doom of earth,
Sent to us all by every rising
Sun. Wisdom is slow, and comes
But late. He who has it is patient;   65
He cannot be hasty to hate or speak,
He must be bold and yet not blind,
Nor ever too craven, complacent, or covetous,
Nor ready to gloat before he wins glory.
The man's a fool who flings his boasts•   70
Hotly to the heavens, heeding his spleen
And not the better boldness of knowledge.
What knowing man knows not the ghostly,
Wastelike end of worldly wealth:
See, already the wreckage is there,   75
The windswept walls stand far and wide,
The storm-beaten blocks besmeared with frost,
The mead-halls• crumbled, the monarchs thrown down
And stripped of their pleasures. The proudest of warriors
Now lie by the wall: some of them war   80
Destroyed; some the monstrous sea bird
Bore over the ocean; to some the old wolf
Dealt out death; and for some dejected
Followers fashioned an earth-cave coffin.
Thus the Maker of men lays waste   85
This earth, crushing our callow mirth,
And the work of old giants stands withered and still.

He who these ruins rightly sees,
And deeply considers this dark twisted life,
Who sagely remembers the endless slaughters   90
Of a bloody past, is bound to proclaim,
        "Where is the war steed? Where/
                        is the warrior? Where is his warlord?
Where now the feasting-places?/

                        Where now the mead-hall pleasures?
Alas, bright cup! Alas, brave knight!
Alas, you glorious princes! All gone,   95
Lost in the night, as you never had lived,
And all that survives you a serpentine wall,
Wondrously high, worked in strange ways.
Mighty spears have slain these men,
Greedy weapons have framed their fate.   100
            These rocky slopes are beaten by storms,
This earth pinned down by driving snow,
By the horror of winter, smothering warmth
In the shadows of night. And the north angrily
Hurls its hailstorms at our helpless heads.   105
Everything earthly is evilly born,
Firmly clutched by a fickle Fate.
Fortune vanishes, friendship vanishes,
Man is fleeting, woman is fleeting,
And all this earth rolls into emptiness."   110

     So says the sage in his heart,/
                    sitting alone with his thought.
It's good to guard your faith,/
                   nor let your grief come forth
Until it cannot call/
                for help, nor help but heed
The path you've placed before it./
                   It's good to find your grace
In God, the heavenly rock/   115
             where rests our every hope.

THE SEAFARER

This tale is true, and mine. It tells
How the sea took me, swept me back
And forth in sorrow and fear and pain,
Showed me suffering in a hundred ships,
In a thousand ports, and in me. It tells   5

Of smashing surf when I sweated in the cold
Of an anxious watch, perched in the bow
As it dashed under cliffs. My feet were cast
In icy bands, bound with frost,
With frozen chains, and hardship groaned   10
Around my heart. Hunger tore
At my sea-weary soul. No man sheltered
On the quiet fairness of earth can feel
How wretched I was, drifting through winter
On an ice-cold sea, whirled in sorrow,   15
Alone in a world blown clear of love,
Hung with icicles. The hailstorms flew.
The only sound was the roaring sea,
The freezing waves. The song of the swan
Might serve for pleasure, the cry of the sea fowl,   20
The croaking of birds instead of laughter,
The mewing of gulls instead of mead•.
Storms beat on the rocky cliffs and were echoed
By icy-feathered terns and the eagle's screams;
No kinsman could offer comfort there,   25
To a soul left drowning in desolation.
          And who could believe, knowing but
The passion of cities, swelled proud with wine
And no taste of misfortune, how often, how wearily,
I put myself back on the paths of the sea.   30
Night would blacken; it would snow from the north;
Frost bound the earth and hail would fall,
The coldest seeds. And how my heart
Would begin to beat, knowing once more
The salt waves tossing and the towering sea!   35
The time for journeys would come and my soul
Called me eagerly out, sent me over
The horizon, seeking foreigners' homes.
          But there isn't a man on earth so proud,
So born to greatness, so bold with his youth,   40
Grown so brave, or so graced by God,
That he feels no fear as the sails unfurl,

Wondering what Fate has willed and will do.
No harps• ring in his heart, no rewards,
No passion for women, no worldly pleasures,   45
Nothing, only the ocean's heave;
But longing wraps itself around him.
Orchards blossom, the towns bloom,
Fields grow lovely as the world springs fresh,
And all these admonish that willing mind   50
Leaping to journeys, always set
In thoughts traveling on a quickening tide.
So summer's sentinel, the cuckoo, sings
In his murmuring voice, and our hearts mourn
As he urges. Who could understand,   55
In ignorant ease, what we others suffer
As the paths of exile stretch endlessly on?
       And yet my heart wanders away,
My soul roams with the sea, the whales'
Home, wandering to the widest corners   60
Of the world, returning ravenous with desire,
Flying solitary, screaming, exciting me
To the open ocean, breaking oaths
On the curve of a wave. Thus the joys of God
Are fervent with life, where life itself   65
Fades quickly into the earth. The wealth
Of the world neither reaches to Heaven nor remains.
No man has ever faced the dawn
Certain which of Fate's three threats
Would fall: illness, or age, or an enemy's   70
Sword, snatching the life from his soul.
The praise the living pour on the dead
Flowers from reputation: plant
An earthly life of profit reaped
Even from hatred and rancor, of bravery   75
Flung in the devil's face, and death
Can only bring you earthly praise
And a song to celebrate a place
With the angels, life eternally blessed
In the hosts of Heaven. The days are gone   80

When the kingdoms of earth flourished in glory;
Now there are no rulers, no emperors,
No givers of gold, as once there were,
When wonderful things were worked among them
And they lived in lordly magnificence. 85
Those powers have vanished, those pleasures are dead.
The weakest survives and the world continues,
Kept spinning by toil. All glory is tarnished.
The world's honor ages and shrinks,
Bent like the men who mold it. Their faces 90
Blanch as time advances, their beards
Wither and they mourn the memory of friends,
The sons of princes, sown in the dust.
The soul stripped of its flesh knows nothing
Of sweetness or sour, feels no pain, 95
Bends neither its hands nor its brain. A brother
Opens his palms and pours down gold
On his kinsman's grave, strewing his coffin
With treasures intended for Heaven, but nothing
Golden shakes the wrath of God 100
For a soul overflowing with sin, and nothing
Hidden on earth rises to Heaven.
    We all fear God. He turns the earth,
He set it swinging firmly in space,
Gave life to the world and light to the sky. 105
Death leaps at fools who forget their God.
He who lives humbly has angels from Heaven
To carry him courage and strength and belief.
A man must conquer pride, not kill it,
Be firm with his fellows, chaste for himself, 110
Treat all the world as the world deserves,
With love or with hate but never with harm,
Though an enemy seek to scorch him in Hell,
Or set the flames of a funeral pyre
Under his lord. Fate is stronger 115
And God mightier than any man's mind.
Our thoughts should turn to where our home is,
Consider the ways of coming there,

Then strive for sure permission for us
To rise to that eternal joy,   120
That life born in the love of God
And the hope of Heaven. Praise the Holy
Grace of Him who honored us,
Eternal, unchanging Creator of earth. Amen.

A WOMAN'S LAMENT

This song of journeys into sorrow
Is mine. I sing it. I alone
Can ravel out its misery, full-grown
When I was, and never worse than now.
The darkness of exile droops on my life.   5
First, my lord went away, sailed
On the tossing waves. I was left in the dawn
Friendless where affection had been. I traveled
Seeking the sun of protection and safety,
Accepting exile as payment for hope.   10
        But the man's family was weaving plans
In the dark, intending to drive us apart
With a wedge the width of the world, condemning
Our love to a living death. I wept.
My new lord sent me to live in the woods,   15
Among the trees, in a land where I knew
No lovers, no friends. So sadness was framed,
For I'd matched myself with a fitting man,
Born to misfortune, blessed with sorrow,
His mind closed to me, mulling on murder.   20
How gaily, how often, we'd fashioned oaths
Defying everything but death to endanger
Our love; now only the words are left
And our friendship's a fable that time has forgotten
And never tells. For my well-belovèd   25
I've been forced to suffer, far and near.
        I was ordered to live in a nest of leaves,
In an earthen cavern under an oak.
I writhe with longing in this ancient hole;

The valleys seem leaden, the hills reared aloft,   30
And the bitter towns all bramble patches
Of empty pleasure. The memory of parting
Rips at my heart. My friends are out there,
Savoring their lives, secure in their beds,
While at dawn, alone, I crawl miserably down   35
Under the oak growing out of my cave.
There I must squat the summer-long day,
There I can water the earth with weeping
For exile and sorrow, for sadness that can never
Find rest from grief nor from the famished   40
Desires that leap at unquenched life.
          May that man be always bent with misery,
With calloused thoughts; may he have to cling
To laughter and smile when sorrow is clamoring
Wild for his blood; let him win his pleasures   45
Unfriended, alone; force him out
Into distant lands—as my lover dwells
In the shade of rocks the storm has frosted,
My downhearted lover, in a desolate hall
Lapped by floods. His suffering drowns him: 50
How can he smother swelling memories
Of a better place? There are few things more bitter
Than awaiting a love who is lost to hope.

WULF AND EADWACER

Wulf may be the female speaker's exiled lover and Eadwacer
her captor husband

My people may have been given a warning:
Will they receive him, if he comes with force?

          It is different for us.

Wulf is on an island, I on another.
An island of forts, surrounded by swamp.   5
That island belongs to bloody barbarians:
Will they receive him, if he comes with force?

It is different for us.

Hope has wandered in exile, with Wulf.
When the rain was cold and my eyes ran red   10
With tears, when heavy arms reached out and took me
And I suffered pleasure and pain. Wulf,
Oh my Wulf, it was hoping and longing for you
That sickened me, starved for the sight of you,
Bent with a despair deeper than hunger.   15

Listen, Eadwacer! The wolf will carry
Our wretched cub to the shade of the wood.
It's easy to smash what never existed,
You and I together.

THE HUSBAND'S MESSAGE

*Spoken by the staff on which the message has been inscribed. The manuscript
is torn; this text is based in part on reconstructions. The runes• of lines 49–
50 may mean, in slightly altered form, either "Follow the sun's path across the
ocean and our's will be joy and the happiness and prosperity of the bright day"
or "Follow the sun's path across the sea to find joy with the man who is waiting
for you."*

A tree grew me; I was green, and wood.
That came first. I was cut and sent
Away from my home, holding wily
Words, carried out on the ocean,
Riding a boat's back. I crossed   5
Stormy seas, seeking the thresholds
Where my master's message was meant to travel
And be known. And now the knotted planks
Of a ship have brought me here, and you
Shall read my lord's heart and hear   10
His soul's thought. I promise a glowing
Faith shall be what you find. Read.

See: this wood has come to make you
Remember the hands that carved it, to take you

Back to the love and the pledges you shared,   15
You two, in that buried time when you both
Could walk unharmed across this festive
Town, the land yours, and you
Each other's. Your people fought, and the feud
Brought him exile. Now he asks you   20
To listen for the sad cuckoo calling
In the grove: when its song has reached the edge
Of the woods, he wants you to come to him over
The waves, letting nothing lead you
Aside and no man living stop you.   25
          Go down to the sea, the gull's home,
And come to a ship that can carry you south,
Away, out on the water to where
Your husband and lord longs for your coming.
Nothing the world can send him, he says   30
Through me, could bring him more delight
Than for Almighty God to grant him you,
And for you and he together to bless
His friends and allies with treasure, with hammered
Bracelets and rings. For though his home   35
Is with strangers, he lives in a lovely land
And is rich: shining gold surrounds him.
And though my master was driven from here,
Rushing madly down to his ship
And onto the sea, alone, only   40
Alive because he fled, and glad
To escape, yet now he is served and followed,
Loved and obeyed by many. He has beaten
Misery: there's nothing more he wants,
Oh prince's daughter, no precious gems,   45
No stallions, no mead-hall• pleasure, no treasure
On earth, but you, you to enjoy
In spite of the ancient threats that parted you.
And I fit together an S and an R,
And E, an A, a W and D,   50
In an oath to prove that your pledge is sacred
To him, and his faith as steady as his heart.

As long as life shall be in him, he'll long
To fulfill the vows and the love you shared.

DEOR

*Wayland, a legendary smith whom Nithad had crippled and enslaved, forged
himself metal wings, killed Nithad's sons, drugged and violated Nithad's
daughter, Beadhild, and flew to safety. Nithad's kingdom was Wermland, now
western Sweden.*

Wermland was misery's home for Wayland
The smith, stubborn even in suffering.
Enduring his exile alone, in longing
And wintry sadness, locked in the snows
Of that northern kingdom when Nithad slit   5
His sinews and trapped a wonderful slave.

    That passed, and so may this.

Her brothers' death meant less to Beadhild
Than the tears she shed for herself, seeing
Her belly sprouting and knowing herself   10
With child, remembering nothing, never
Any man's bride but bearing fruit.

    That passed, and so may this.

We've heard that rape in a thousand songs,
And in the infinite love which left old Nithad   15
Tossing sleepless on a bed of regret.

    That passed, and so may this.

And Theodoric, once thirty years
The Maerings' ruler, and now no more.

    That passed, and so may this.   20

We've heard them sing the story of Ermric's
Fierceness, who ruled the Gothic folk
Like a savage wolf. His throne was set
In twisted hearts, and hundreds of warriors
Languished in futile dreams of his fall   25
While waiting, helpless, for what was sure to come.

　　　That passed, and so may this.

They sat in chains, sorrowful, empty
Of everything life had held, lost
In thoughts of their endless pain. And yet   30
They could have followed the silent footsteps
Of God, walking over the world,
Shedding mercy and grace to many
And dropping sorrow on a few lost souls.
Of myself I will say that once I sang   35
For the Héodénings, and held a place
In my master's heart. My name was Deor.
I sang in my good lord's service through many
Winters•, until Heórrend won
My honors away, struck his harp•   40
And stole my place with a poet's skill.

　　　That passed, and so may this.

THE RUIN

*Ancient Roman wreckage, perhaps Bath. Lines 12–19a and 42b–49 are
fragmentary; the manuscript was partly destroyed by fire.*

Fate has smashed these wonderful walls,
This broken city, has crumbled the work
Of giants. The roofs are gutted, the towers
Fallen, the gates ripped off, frost
In the mortar, everything molded, gaping,   5
Collapsed. The earth has clutched at rulers
And builders, a hundred generations rotting

In its rigid hands. These red-stained stones,
Streaked with gray, stood while governors
And kingdoms dissolved into dust, and storms   10
Crashed on them; they were broad and high, and they fell.
Still standing . . . . all heaped up,
Many in . . . .
Savagely ground into powder . . . .
. . . . they shone   15
. . . . cunningly worked old creation . . . .
. . . . ringed with crusts of mud,
Their minds . . . .
Determined, strong-hearted men wove
The walls together with beaten wire.   20
It was a shining city, filled with bathhouses,
With towering gables, with the shouts of soldiers,
With dozens of rousing drinking halls,
Until Fate's strength was swung against it.
The riches dried away, pestilence   25
Came, the crowds of brave men were dead;
Their forts and camps crumbled to the ground,
And the city, with all its idols and temples,
Decayed to these ruins, its buildings rotted,
Its red-stoned arches splitting brick   30
From brick. And the ruined site sank
To a heap of tumbled stones, where once
Cheerful, strutting warriors flocked,
Golden armor gleaming, giddy
With wine; here was wealth, silver,   35
Gems, cattle, land, in the crowning
City of a far-flung kingdom. There were buildings
Of stone, where steaming currents threw up
Surging heat; a wall encircled
That brightness, with the baths inside at the glowing   40
Heart. Life was easy and lush.
They'd make the warm streams pour over
Old gray stones . . . .
. . . . until

The rounded pools grew hot   45
. . . . where the baths were
And it's . . . .
. . . . a kingly thing.
A house . . . . . . a city . . . .

Heroic Poems

Even in times documented by written records, Old English society was warlike, and its people always valued heroic• poetry. When Old English poets recounted stories that celebrate the virtues of Christian saints (the heroes of the Christian era), they composed them, too, in heroic form. Of particular interest is *Judith,* a retelling of an Old Testament book from the Septuagint version of the Bible, which is found in the manuscript containing *Beowulf.* The Old English Judith is both a biblical figure and a hero like Beowulf. Just as an Anglo-Saxon warrior serves his king, Judith serves the "All-powerful King" (92) and asks for "Victory and true faith" (89). *Elene* recounts the legend of the finding of the True Cross by the mother of the emperor Constantine the Great. Although the main portion of *Elene* is not translated here, the opening has been included to provide an example of heroic poetry about saints and a sample of the poet Cynewulf's work. This fragment focuses on Constantine, the king who "led and protected his people bravely / And well" (11–12) and his visit from a "shining / Angel from Heaven" (76–77).

The most celebrated poem of the Old English canon is *Beowulf.* The fragmentary poem *The Battle of Finnsburh* appeals to the same heroic values and comitatus ethos. It is the story of the Danish

king Hnæf and his brother Hengest, who, on a visit to their sister
Hildeburh, are attacked by her husband, Finn, ruler of the Frisians.
This fragment presents a vivid picture of heroic behavior:

So now awake, my loyal warriors!
Lift your shields, summon your courage,
Aim your spears forward, stand firm, be bold!

(10–12)

Because some scholars have identified this Hengest with the Hengest
who led the invasion of England in 449, the poem has attracted the
interest of historians.

The *Anglo-Saxon Chronicle* is mainly a prose work, but some docu-
mentary poems are interspersed. *The Battle of Brunanburh* is a pane-
gyric on the heroism of King Athelstan and his younger brother
Edmund. Men seem to fight for a new ideal, England, as well as
for their lord. The poem uses the theme of the Beasts of Battle, de-
scribing a historical battle in the mythical terms of older heroic
poetry. *The Anglo-Saxon Chronicle: A.D. 975* is a brief poem that focuses
on the death of King Edgar: "In this year ended the earthly plea-
sures / Of Edgar" (1–2).

Another poem that commemorates a historical battle is *The Battle
of Maldon,* a fragment that commemorates the fight of the ealdor-
man• Byrtnoth against the Danes. We have included the *Anglo-Saxon
Chronicle* entry for the year 991 so that readers can see the difference
between the same story told in spare prose and in heroic verse. At
the end of the fragment, Byrtwold gives a ringing statement of the
comitatus ideal:

Our minds must be stronger, our hearts
Braver, our courage higher, as our numbers
Shrink:

(312–314)

JUDITH

*Following the Latin Vulgate text of the apocryphal book of Judith — the
standard English Bible is translated from a rather different Hebrew version than
the Septuagint, on which the Vulgate is based — the poem tells of Holofernes,*

Nebuchadnezzar's general, who invades Judea and besieges the city of Bethulia.
Judith, a beautiful Jewish girl, voluntarily enters Holofernes' camp, knowing
the general's susceptibility. We do not have the complete poem. What we do
have opens with the Assyrian feast that precedes her coming to his tent.

A technical note: observe the high frequency of hypermetric• lines. Only
one Old English poem, according to Elliott van Kirk Dobbie, has a higher
proportion of such expanded lines, and no Old English poem — other than
that tour de force The Riming Poem — *contains more frequent rhymes and*
near-rhymes• than Judith.

. . . . and was sure of
Grace, here in this wide-reaching/
                          world. His help was waiting,
Heaven's Glorious King,/
                Lord of Creation, His kindness
And protection; when she needed Him most,/
                       danger closest and most real,
He alone was her guard,/   5
             the exalted Ruler of the world,
Extending His hand to defend her,/
                 rewarding the unshaken faith
She had always shown Him. And then,/
                  it is told, Holofernes
Commanded his people to lay out/
              a feast, with wine and magnificent
Dishes, strange and wonderfully/
            made. And the Assyrian lord
Ordered his noblest lieutenants/   10
           to attend him; they hurried to obey,
The best of his warriors, came/
         when their mighty leader called them
To his side. The day of that feast/
          was the fourth Judith had spent
In his camp; he had never seen the wise
And radiant virgin, but that day he sent for her.

   They began their feast, bold and arrogant   15
Warriors, Holofernes' companions,

As wicked as their leader. Shining bowls
Were carried back and forth/
                             along the benches, and cups
Were filled to the rim; the famous soldiers
Who drank them were already doomed, but their terrible   20
Lord suspected nothing. When the wine
Rose in him their chieftain roared and shouted
With triumph, bellowed so loud that his fierce
Voice carried far beyond
His tent, his wild pleasure was heard   25
Everywhere. And he demanded, over and over,
That his men empty their cups, drink deep.
        Thus the evil prince, haughty
Giver of rings, soaked his soldiers
In wine, the whole day through,/   30
                       drenched them till their heads swam
And they fell to the ground, all drunk,/
                    lay as though death had struck them
Down, drained of their sense./
               So their leader commanded them
To be served, master of men,/
              until the darkness of night
Drew near. And then, his soul/
              corrupted by sin, he ordered
The blessèd Judith brought to his bed   35
At once, adorned with bracelets and golden
Rings. His servants ran, hearing
Their lord's commands, leader of mail-shirted
Men: in a whirl of noise they marched
To the guesthouse, where that knowing virgin awaited them,   40
And quickly prepared herself, that radiant woman.
Then they hurried her off, Holofernes'
Soldiers, to their master's towering tent;
There, at night, their mighty ruler,
Hated by the Lord, would rest, bloated   45
With wine. And around their leader's great bed
Hung a shimmering net, golden

And beautiful, so his evil eyes, prince
Of warriors, could see everything, watching
His door, but none of the sons of men   50
Could know he was staring except when he called
Some brave lieutenant, proven in battle,
To come close, and whispered secret/
                              words. They came, hurrying
The wise virgin to his bed,/
                              then went where their lord awaited them
And announced that his will had been done,/   55
                              the holy woman led
To his couch. The famous conqueror/
                              of cities and towns smiled
And laughed, hearing them, his heart/
                              joyful, thinking how Judith
Could be smeared with his filth, stained/
                              with dishonor. But our Glorious Savior,
Guardian of the world, Lord/
                              and Master of men, refused him,
Kept her safe from such sin./   60
                        Then Holofernes and a crowd
Of soldiers came staggering to his tent, hunting for
Their evil master's bed,/
                        where their ruler would give up life
And glory all at once,/
                        in a single night, mighty
In battle, a proud leader,/
                        and cruel, coming to the end
He'd sought, had striven to reach,/   65
                        while his life lasted, while the earth
Was beneath him and the sky above./
                              He entered, their great general,
And fell across his bed,/
                        so full of wine that his brain
Was numb. Quickly, his followers left
His chamber, their own feet unsteady, having led
Him home, their breaker of pledges, liar,   70

Tyrant and devil, for the last time.
Watching him fall, our Savior's glorious
Servant, Judith, struggled to see
How his unclean soul could best be freed
From his foul and sinful body before   75
His senses returned. And then our Lord's
Faithful virgin slowly drew out
His battle-hard sword, unsheathed that sharp
Blade with her right hand, and raised
Her voice toward Heaven and the Savior of us all,   80
Calling on God with these words:
      "Lord of creation and creatures, Spirit
Of our comfort and our joy, Almighty Son,
Glorious Trinity, grant me Your mercy,
Your help! My heart is beating wildly,   85
My head reels, confused, troubled
By its own doubts. Send me,/
                oh Ruler of Heaven and Earth,
Victory and true faith;/
            let me kill this vicious king
Of sin and murder with his battle-sharp/
                  sword. Mighty Prince,
Let me be saved. My soul/   90
           has never needed Your grace
More than now, than here./
            All-powerful King, make me
Able to work Your vengeance,/
              as my heart longs to; let me
Celebrate Your greatness, Your glory."/
                 Then the Judge of us all, in highest
Heaven, filled her with perfect/
             courage—as all men find
When they come to Him, seeking/   95
               His help with knowing hearts
And true belief. Hope/
          and joy cleansed her soul,
And her saintly heart exulted./

Taking the sleeping pagan•

By the hair she slowly drew him/
toward her, with both hands,

Watching him, until that evil
Leader of men lay as she wanted him,   100
Carefully placed where his God-cursed life
Lay at her mercy. Then Judith struck at him,
The hated robber, with his shining sword,
Swung it so well that it cut his neck
Half through, and he opened and closed his eyes,   105
And lay unconscious, drunken, bleeding.
He was still alive: with a fierce stroke
She struck at the heathen• dog again,
And his head leaped from his body, went rolling
Along the floor. Life flew   110
From his stinking corpse, and his soul fled
Deep into Hell's darkness, condemned
To eternal torment, chained into agony,
Slimy serpents wound around it,
Imprisoned forever in the burning flames,   115
Suffering endlessly. And nothing would ever
Free him, release him from the darkness burning
All around him, loosen the snakes from his throat:
He could know no hope, only writhe
Forever without end in that shadowy world.   120

    Then Judith had won fame, earned glory
In war, granted her by God, Lord
Of Heaven, victory sent from on high.
And the wise virgin quickly dropped
Holofernes' bloody head   125
Into the sack her female slave, a girl
With fair hair and skin, used
To carry food for them both; Judith
Handed the bloody bundle to her faithful
Servant, thoughtful and quiet of tongue,   130
To carry home. Then lady and slave,

Both of them bold and quick, hurriedly
Left the tent and walked, proud
And triumphant, through the Assyrian camp,
Till they saw, bright and clear, the beautiful   135
Walls of Bethulia, gleaming in the sun.
They walked swiftly, two ring-adorned women,
Walked swiftly and straight until, happy
And blessed, they reached the back gate
Of the city. Warriors lined the wall,   140
Watchful men guarding their homes,
Sorrowful, protecting their stronghold, as Judith
Had ordered, addressing her people before
She left, that far-seeing virgin, on her dangerous
Journey. And now their beloved had returned.   145
Quickly, Judith called for someone
To come to them, a warrior from that far-flung town
To hurry down and open Bethulia's
Gate and admit them. And she spoke of the victory
Her people had won: 150
　　　　"I can tell you wonders:
Praise them. Fear and sorrow can now be
Forgotten. God, our Glorious King,
Is pleased with this people and has told His pleasure
Across the wide world, declared that glory   155
And triumph will be yours, honor and fame
To repay the wrongs and afflictions you have known."
　　　　Hearing how the holy maiden spoke,
Still standing outside their high walls,
The citydwellers were joyful. Cheering   160
Soldiers, merchants, men and women
Together, young and old, crowded
Toward the gate, flowed through the town by the thousands,
Rushing to greet the saintly girl,
The Lord's servant. And everyone in that noisy,   165
Happy town knew delight,
Learning that Judith had returned, come back
To her home and her people. Quickly, humbly,

They swung wide the gate and let her enter.
    Then that gold-adorned virgin, wise and brave,   170
Ordered her servant to open the bundle
Held in her careful hands, and show
Holofernes' bloody head—
Proof and witness of the battle she had fought
And won. And she raised her voice to them all: 175
    "See, leaders of this people, triumphant
Warriors, see this heathen's skull,
Lifeless, ugly, Holofernes'
Head, he who of all men
Brought us the greatest pain, a butcher   180
Who meant to continue his slaughter, our torment,
But God ended his life, gave death
To an enemy who had lived only to injure us.
The Lord guided my hand, helped me
To kill him. Citizens, soldiers: I ask you   185
All, every shield-bearing man,
To prepare for battle. When the Lord of creation,
Our merciful King, sends the first
Bright gleaming light from the East, carry
Your swords and shields against the Assyrians,   190
Bear your gleaming mail shirts, your silver
Helmets, to the heart of their camp, and kill
Their leaders, cut them down with your glittering
Blades. Those deaths are already written:
Almighty God has condemned your enemies,   195
Granted you glory in battle, God
Himself, and sent you signs by my hand."
    Quickly, the bold Jews made themselves
Ready, prepared to fight: marching
With their banners waving above them, leaders   200
And led, brave men all, they headed
Straight for the Assyrian camp, left
Their holy city as dawn broke.
Their shields rang out in the darkness, and the
Wolf, deep in the wood, exulted,   205
And the bloodthirsty raven, both of them knowing

That men meant to spread a feast
For their empty bellies. And behind them flew
The damp-feathered eagle, dark and hungry
For human meat, singing a war song   210
Through his horny beak. And the warriors marched on,
Their hollow shields held high, heroes
Hurrying to war, seeking heathen
Invaders, strangers in their land, who'd mocked
And abused them, once. Now the Jews   215
Were approaching the Assyrian camp, carrying
Jewish flags, and fighting would more
Than repay pagan taunts. The Hebrew
Archers bent their horn-tipped bows
And a stream of poisoned arrows dropped   220
From the sky, a bold hailstorm of bitter
Darts. The angry Jews shouted
With a roar, and sent spears and javelins
Flying through the air. Their hearts were wild,
Their hands firm and strong, as one   225
By one they hunted the drunken invaders
Down, shook them awake, and killed them,
Their ancient enemies. Bright-shining swords
Swept out of sheaths, battle-hard blades
Bit into Assyrian flesh, struck down   230
Scheming warriors, hated invaders.
They spared none of them, rich and poor
Fell together, man after once-living
Man, as Jewish soldiers caught them.

      All through the morning the Jews advanced   235
And their enemies fell back, fleeing from Hebrew
Might, till at last the retreat reached
Deep into the Assyrian camp, and the officers
Heard how Jewish swords were sweeping
An army away. They hurried to the oldest   240
And noblest among them, broke in on lords
And leaders, lying in sodden sleep,
And shaking with fear described the morning's

Slaughter, announced their disastrous news.
Then doomed generals jumped from their beds,   245
Wrenching sleep from their eyes, and the whole
Weary, dejected crowd pushed
Through the camp, came rushing to their evil lord,
Holofernes, and stood in front of
His tent, hoping to tell him, before   250
Jewish soldiers announced themselves,
How war had struck. They were sure their prince
Was asleep, inside, their harsh, cruel
Lord, with Judith sharing his silken
Bed, battle-hard rake and beautiful   255
Virgin, coupled in his sheets. None of them
Dared to wake him, trembled at the thought
Of entering his tent, asking how the woman
Had been, God's shining virgin,
Graced with His love. The Jews came closer,   260
Avenging ancient insults at the point
Of their gleaming knives, blood-sharp blades
Hacking a furious victory, repaying
A savage debt: Assyrian fame
And Assyrian pride were bent and broken,   265
When that day was done. And still the soldiers
Stood in front of the tent, excited,
Helpless, their hearts grim. Then suddenly,
With a single voice, they began to shriek
And gnash their teeth, fear opening   270
Their jaws and forcing suffering/
                              out. Glory and courage,
Riches and honor, all/
                         had ended. They meant to rouse
Their prince; they could not. At last, but too late,
One of them, driven by fright, found
Courage enough to approach the tent   275
And enter. There, alone in his bed,
Lay his lord and master, headless, his blood
Drained out, his life gone elsewhere, an empty

Corpse. The Assyrian shivered with fear
And fell to the ground, tearing at his hair   280
And his clothes, his brain choked with sorrow;
Calling to his sad-hearted companions, standing
Outside, waiting for some word, he declared:
      "Here is the proof: our death has been spoken,
Ruin and death are pushing closer   285
And closer, their time and ours/
              has come: we will die together,
All of us, fall on our enemies'/
              swords. Here lies our lord,
Our leader, our prince, slain,/
           his head cut from his body."
      They threw away their weapons,/
             turned and wearily began
To run. The mighty Hebrew army   290
Followed, tracking them down, fighting
Across that field of victory till Assyrian
Bodies lay everywhere, waiting
For wolves to take their pleasure, for bloodthirsty
Vultures to rejoice. The Jews slew   295
Most of them; whoever was able ran,
And running, lived. But Judith's people
Pursued them, filled with triumph and the glory
Of God, victorious in the Almighty's will,
Brave and bold in His service, their swords   300
Cutting a path in front of them, cracking
Assyrian shields, smashing defending
Armor. Bowmen and swordsmen, and all
The Jews, fought like giants, angry,
Eager to shove their spears through Assyrian   305
Hearts. More of their hated enemies
Died than lived, and most of the leaders,
Nobles and lords, fell in the sand.
A handful escaped, left Judea
Alive, came back to their home. Brave,   310
Once, they surrendered to fear, fled,

And turned into steaming corpses. And the Jews
Stripped the hated bodies, plucked
Lifeless enemies of their dark, gleaming
Helmets, their swords and daggers and hammered   315
Armor, carried away bloody
Treasures. Guarding their country against
Its ancient invader, Judea's soldiers
Had won a glorious victory, conquered
And killed in battle. Of all living men   320
Most hated, the Assyrians now slept where life
Had left them. And the Jews, sublimest of peoples,
Stately and proud, gathered in pagan
Riches, worked for a month of days
Carrying weapons and gold-covered armor,   325
Tested swords and silvered mail shirts,
To their shining city, Bethulia, treasure
Greater than wise men can imagine or words
Can tell, all of it won in combat
By brave warriors, under banners swung   330
On high with Judith's wisdom, sent
Into battle as that bold virgin advised.
And her skill was rewarded: they brought her, brave men
Gladly surrendering what was theirs, everything
Holofernes had owned, every   335
Precious treasure that arrogant/
                   master of men had plundered
From across the world, every/
                  golden cup and shining
Jewel, once hidden in his family/
                  vaults, brought her, that quick-witted,
Radiant woman, his sword,/
                  his bloody helmet, and the red-gold
Armor he'd worn to war./   340
                  And Judith told them she'd done
Nothing, except as God/
                  had willed; all glory was His,
Except as He meant her to have it,/

here in this world and then
In Heaven, the most glorious of rewards,/
earned only by faith
In Him alone. She never/
doubted that final reward,
Her soul had always longed for it./   345
May the glory of our beloved Lord
Endure for ever and ever,/
Who made sky and air
And this great earth, and all/
the raging seas, and the joys
Of Heaven, made them in His endless mercy.

ELENE

Excerpt: lines 1–147 of a 1,321-line poem

The turning circle of years had spun
Through the world's winters•, in the way men count,
Two hundred and three times, and then
Still thirty more, since Almighty God,
The King of Glory, had been born on this middle-   5
Earth of ours, light for the faithful
In human form. And Constantine
Had been emperor for six years, had ruled
In Rome, a battle-hard leader, a proven
Soldier raised to the imperial throne.   10
And he led and protected his people bravely
And well. King and kingdom grew strong
And mighty; he was a just ruler
Who defended his warriors. God made him
Famous and powerful, and many men   15
Across the wide world rejoiced, and took heart,
For when he raised his weapons his enemies
Were utterly destroyed. They declared war,
Prepared to fight. The Huns and Hergoths
Gathered together a mighty army,   20

Joined by the bold Franks and Hugas.
They were brave men,*
Ready for battle. Their spears gleamed
Like their woven mail-shirts. Lifting their shields
High, they shouted, clearly showing   25
They meant to fight united as one.
They marched forward. A wolf in the woods
Howled a war-song, proclaiming slaughter.
And following after, the damp-winged eagle
Sang on high. Sweeping down   30
From high mountain slopes came the greatest host
Of armed invaders the King of the Huns
Could possibly put together, drawn
From inhabited places all around.
      They surged forward, forming troops   35
And squadrons, until they came to foreign
Lands, along the banks of the Danube,
And there by the swirling waters they camped,
The bold spearsmen. The roaring throng
Meant to destroy the rule of Rome,   40
Crush it with their hordes. The Roman garrison
Saw them come. And the emperor ordered
Every soldier he had to hurry
And buckle on armor, make himself fit
For the flight of arrows, prepare to fight   45
In open fields. Famous warriors,
The Romans were ready almost at once,
Weapons in hand, although their army
Was smaller than the masses of assembled Huns.
They rode around their leader, shields   50
Clanging, war-wood resounding, then marched
Out to battle. Ravens croaked
On high, black and baleful. Trumpets
And heralds called, horses stamped,
As the army went forward. They marched in formation,   55

---

*Although this is only half a standard line, there is no indication in the
manuscript that anything is missing.

On battle alert. But the emperor was frightened,
Filled with fear, seeing the vast
Hordes of barbarians, Huns and Hergoths,
Gathered together at the boundaries of Rome,
The banks of the river teeming with a force   60
Too large to be counted. The Roman emperor's
Heart was heavy, knowing his own
Army was far too small to defend
The kingdom; his soldiers would be overcome
By superior numbers. Then his men camped   65
For the night at the edge of the river, circled
Around the emperor, having first made sure
How their enemy's positions were settled and arranged.
     And then, as the emperor lay there, surrounded
By his soldiers, the man of many victories   70
Fell asleep, and dreamed he saw
A gleaming vision in the shape of a man,
Dazzling bright. But he did not know him,
This being wholly unlike anything
He'd ever seen in his life. The emperor   75
Jumped up, startled from his sleep. And the shining
Angel from Heaven immediately spoke,
And called him by name. And the darkness disappeared.
     "Oh emperor, the King of Angels, Almighty
Master of Fate, has pledged you His   80
All-ruling protection. Have no fear,
Despite threatening barbarians and the fierce
Fighting to come. Trust in Heaven
And in God Almighty, who will give you His help,
And a sign of victory." As the holy envoy   85
Had ordered, the emperor grew ready, opened
His heart, and looked up, as the messenger commanded,
The faithful angel. And high in Heaven
He saw the tree of glory, hung
With gold and treasures, gleaming with jewels,   90
And on the glowing tree he could read,
In bright, bold letters: "This is the sign
With which you will overcome your enemies,

Defeat their armies." Then the light vanished,
Swept to the skies, and the angel with it,   95
Back into Heaven. And the emperor's heart
Rejoiced, and his fear vanished, lord
Of men, for the beautiful vision he had seen.
          Then Emperor Constantine, prince among princes,
Giver of rings, commanded an image   100
Of Christ's cross to be made, as quickly
As the work could be done, shaped like the sign
He'd seen in Heaven, the glorious king,
The vision so recently revealed to his eyes.
And then, exactly as dawn was breaking,   105
He roused his army, ready for battle,
And ordered that the image of that holy tree,
The beacon of God, be carried in the forefront
Into the enemy ranks. Bugles blared
As the Romans advanced. Ravens rejoiced,   110
And the damp-winged eagle watched from above,
As the bloodshed began. The wood-dwelling wolf
Howled his song. And battle-terror
Reigned. Shields cracked, soldiers
Pushed forward, swords were swung, and men   115
Died as arrows dropped from above.
Barbed showers fell on those doomed
Fighters, fierce spears hit their shields,
Angry darts from a raging enemy,
Hurled through the air by powerful hands.   120
But the soldiers held firm, advanced in formation,
Steadily forward, smashing shields
With their broad-edged swords. Then that beacon was raised
As a sign of triumph, and victory songs
Roared out. Gold helmets and spears gleamed   125
Across the battlefield. And the heathens• were dying,
Given no quarter. And the armies of the Hun
Broke and ran, as the Roman emperor
Ordered the sign of that holy tree
Raised on high. The hardy barbarians   130
Ran for their lives. Many were killed.

Many barely escaped from that field
Of battle. Some, just half alive,
Hid in the hills and the high mountains,
Behind cliffs, in places they knew   135
Near the Danube. And some ended
Their lives, drowned in the river's waters.
          And then the Romans rejoiced in their hearts,
Chasing after their enemies till evening
Fell, and the day ended. Their spears   140
Flew like dragons. The host was cut down,
Their shield-carrying enemies. Not many of the Hunnish
Hordes came home after that battle.
And no one doubted that victory had come
From the Lord Almighty, the Ruler of Heaven,   145
Through His holy tree, brought to the emperor
In token of that day's glorious work.

THE BATTLE OF FINNSBURH

A manuscript fragment

          . . . Are the roof-gables burning?"
King Hnaef, new to battle, answered him:
"No dawn is breaking, no dragon is abroad,
And the roof gables of this hall are not on fire.
But our enemy is approaching: ravens croak,   5
The gray wolf howls, and war-wood will sing
When spears hit shields. The cloud-covered moon
Rolls through the sky. Evil deeds
Will be done, and this people's anger will quicken.
So now awake, my loyal warriors!   10
Lift your shields, summon your courage,
Aim your spears forward, stand firm, be bold!"
          Gold-clad soldiers arose, took up
Their weapons. Then Sigferth and Eaha, lordly
Warriors, drew their swords and stood   15
At one door, and Ordlaf and Guthlaf at the other,
And Hengest himself followed behind them.

And Guthere was still arguing with Garulf,
Trying to keep that good man, armored
And ready, from attacking the doors, now   20
That a strong-hearted enemy was waiting to kill him.
But bold as he was, Garulf demanded
The name of the warrior holding the door.
   "Sigferth!" was the answer, "Prince of the Sedgan,
Known the world over! I've fought my way   25
Through a host of battles. Come take your destiny
Here at my hands, if you want to seek it."
   Then murderous blows could be heard in that hall,
And pointed shields, in heroes' hands,
Were split apart, and the floor shook,   30
And Garulf, Guthlaf's son, was over-
Come, and fell, the first of those fighters
Who'd lived on earth to be dead, but many
More lay beside him. And brown-black ravens
Hovered overhead. Light was flashing   35
From swords as if all of Finnsburh was on fire.
No battle I've ever heard of could boast•
Sixty better warriors, and no giver
Of sweet mead• was better repaid for his gifts
Than was Hnaef, that night, by all his young soldiers.   40
They fought for five days, and not one defender
Fell, but they stood and protected the doors.
   Then a wounded hero staggered away,
Declaring his mail shirt broken to bits,
His war coat useless, and his helmet pierced.   45
And then the leader of that people immediately
Asked if the soldiers could survive their wounds,
And which of the young warriors . . . .

THE BATTLE OF BRUNANBURH

Anglo-Saxon Chronicle: A.D. *937*

This was the year when Athelstan, king
Of Wessex, prince among earls and patron

Of heroes, and his noble brother, Edmund,
Hacked a lifelong glory from a battle
Near Brunanburh. They shattered the phalanx•,   5
Their swords splintered the linden shields,
And the sons of Edward followed their father,
Proved the blood they had tested in battle
Before, defending their land and their homes
Against every invader. The enemy ran,   10
All the Scotch and the shipborne Vikings,
Ran or drowned in blood, dropped
To a landlocked fate as the glorious sun
Went gliding over the earth like a candle
In God's broad palm, blowing sublimely   15
Across the sky and dipping calmly
To darkness and night. The dead lay piled
Where the spears had left them, Vikings and Scots,
Tired, now, of the struggle and wanting
Only to rest. All the battle   20
Became the Wessex cavalry endlessly
Hunting a broken enemy, their honed
And sparkling blades striking home
In fugitives' backs. No Mercian refused
To aim his sword at any man   25
Who'd shared a sail with Anlaf, shipped
Himself across a stormy sea
To a bloody port. Five young princes
Pitched their beds on the battleground
And would never awake, and seven of Anlaf's   30
Earls, and a host of invaders, Viking
And Scotch. Anlaf himself fought
His way to the prow of a ship, he
And a tiny band, forced to flee;
They pressed to sea on a dull brown tide   35
That floated the king to safety. Nor
Did the old one, Constantine, trailing
Defeat behind him all the way north,
Find exultation following his steps
Or boasts• on his lips; he left his kinsmen   40

And friends scattered over the field,
Butchered to silence, and abandoned his son
On the heaps of the slain, an untried soldier
Cut into failure. No, the crafty
Gray-beard had no need to be vain, and no more   45
Had Anlaf: watching their wreck of an army
Nothing welled up into laughter
Or pride that, after amusing themselves
With Edward's sons, they'd proved that they
And theirs were England's best for the job   50
Of battle, the crashing of standards, the thrust
Of spears, the cut and slash of dagger
And sword. They fled in their mail-clad ships,
The bloodstained Northmen, over a deep and noisy
Sea to Dublin, back again   55
To Ireland, ashamed, disgraced. But those ashes
Of defeat were the sweetest taste of victory
In the brothers' mouths, Wessex king
And Wessex prince, returning home
Together. They left a gift of dismembered   60
Corpses to the horny beak of the black-plumaged
Raven, and the gray-feathered eagle, splashed white
On his tail, to the greedy war-hawk and the gray-flanked
Forest wolf, a feast of carcasses
For lovers of carrion meat. No carnage   65
Had ever been bloodier, in any battle
Fought anywhere on this island, say the books
Of the old philosophers, not since the Angles
And Saxons arrived in England out of
The East, brave men trying a broad   70
And dangerous sea, daring warriors
Who swept away the Britons•, seized
The land and made it theirs alone.

ANGLO-SAXON CHRONICLE: A.D. 975

In this year ended the earthly pleasures
Of Edgar, king of England, who sought

A different and lovelier light and left
This worthless life for one more lasting.
And all men everywhere on earth, and in England,   5
Properly schooled in the science of numbers,
Know that the king, the young ring-giver•,
Left the world and his life in the month
Named after Julius, and on its eighth day.
And after him his half-grown son   10
Received the kingdom, and Edward became
The chief of England's earls, and her king.

THE BATTLE OF MALDON

Anglo-Saxon Chronicle, A.D. 991; the beginning and end of the poem are
missing
"In this year Olaf [Tryggvason, later king of Norway] came to
Folkestone with ninety-three ships, and plundered the outskirts, and
then went on to Sandwich, and proceeded from there to Ipswich,
and completely overran it, and then went on to Maldon, and there
Ealdorman• Byrtnoth with his army came out to meet him, and
fought against him. And they killed the ealdorman, and were masters
of the battlefield. And, later, peace was made with him, and the king
acted as his sponsor when the bishop confirmed him."

               . . . was broken,
He ordered a warrior to free the horses,
Whip them away, then stride into war
With his mind on his hands and his heart high.
And Offa's kinsman discovered, watching   5
Retreat cut off, that cowards had no place
With Byrtnoth; he released his beloved falcon,
And as it flew to the woods walked toward the battle,
An open promise of courage that everyone
Saw; no one could doubt his pride   10
Or his youth. And Edric was there, eager
To follow his lord, stepping forward
With a ready spear. For as long as his hands
Could hold a sword and a shield he swung them

Bravely, sealing his boast• that battle   15
Would find him fighting beside his chief.
      Then Byrtnoth rallied his men, riding
And shouting, showing his soldiers where
To station themselves, and how to stand,
Commanding the rows of shields to keep straight   20
And strong and to hold off fear. And when
His troops stood firm he slipped off his stallion
And posted himself in the center, where the men
Of his household were grouped and his heart led him.
      Then the Viking herald hailed them, standing   25
On the opposite shore and bellowing his message
Across to the English earl, the loud
Threats of the Norse and Danish raiders:
"The bold seamen have sent me here
To tell you: if you want protection, quickly   30
Pay its price—and you'd better buy off
Our spears with tribute before we send them
Smashing against your shields. But gold,
If you have it, will save you; we'll sell you peace.
And if you who make decisions, who lead   35
These people, decide to ransom their lives,
These seamen will freely furnish you quiet
And safety. Buy security from us
And we'll turn back to our ships, put your treasure aboard,
Set out to sea on the freshening tide   40
And leave you our absence—your best protection."
      Then Byrtnoth spoke, raising his shield
And shaking his spear, hurling an angry
And resolute answer back in their faces:
      "Listen, sailors. Can you hear what we say?   45
We offer a tribute of tempered steel,
Javelins and spears with poisoned points,
Weapons and armor you'll wear only
In death. Messenger, this is your answer:
Tell your leaders the unlucky news   50
That this earl and his army don't shake at their boasts,
But will stand and defend their homes and fields

And all this land and these people, who belong
To Ethelred, my king. You pagans• die
When the swords swing. And how could I let you   55
Return to your ships burdened with treasure
Yet without the fighting you came for, wasting
Your trouble in traveling so far to our country?
Wealth doesn't drop from our hands, here.
We forge our peace on the points of our spears   60
And they're yours for the asking: blood, not gold."
       Then he ordered the English shields to stand
In a line along the bank. Neither
Army could reach the other: after
The tide ebbed, the waters whirled   65
As the current swept down against them. It felt like
An endless waiting for steel to clash,
The English blades, and the Danes, drawn up
In battle array on the banks of the Panta.
Neither could injure the other; only   70
A handful died where arrows fell.
       Finally the tide drained out: the rows
Of waiting Danes rushed to the ford.
But Byrtnoth ordered the bridge held
And sent a battle-hardened guard: 75
Wulfstan, Ceola's son and born
To bravery. As the first sailor came forward
He swung his javelin and the Dane dropped.
And Alfhere and Maccus stood beside him,
Unafraid, a pair of warriors   80
Who would never have fled from the ford but kept it
Swung shut on the Danish swords, held it
While their hands could hold their spears. But the Danes
Learned quickly, and seeing clearly the kind
Of defenders they'd found fell back, began   85
A sly deceit. The hated strangers
Begged for permission to land, a place
To lead their men safely across
Into battle.
       And Byrtnoth's pride said yes.   90

He began to call over the swift, cold water,
And his soldiers listened:
                    "The ford is open,
Cross it and come to us. Quickly. Only
God holds the secret of victory."   95
            So, the sea wolves, the Norse sailors,
No longer afraid of the stream, crossed west
On the Panta, carried their shields over shining
Water and brought seamen and spears to land.
Byrtnoth and his warriors waited to meet them,   100
Ready, their linden shields linked rim
To rim in a wall raised on their arms
And firm. Then fighting hung on a sword blade,
Glory in battle; the time had come
For fate to pluck out ripened lives.   105
The armies shouted, and above them the eagles
And ravens circled, greedy for carrion.
Then sharp-honed steel flew from their hands,
Fine-ground spears; and the bows hummed,
And blades thudded on upraised shields.   110
            The charge was savage: soldiers fell
On every side, and lay where they dropped.
Wulfmar was wounded and slept on the bloody
Field, Byrtnoth's nephew, killed
By the sudden sweep of a hooked broadsword.   115
But the seamen were paid in kind. I heard
That Edward offered a proper tribute,
Struck a Dane so sharply that he fell
At his feet and fought no more. For which
His chief thanked the chamberlain, when the chance   120
Came.
            So they stood, neither
Yielding, every warrior eagerly
Planning another's death, his point
The first to show eternity to a mortal   125
Soul. The slaughtered were thick on the ground.
And they stood firm. Byrtnoth held them,
Ordered every thought on the battle

And the glory of beating back the Danes.
A brave warrior raised his weapons   130
And came at Byrtnoth, waving his shield.
The earl strode as boldly toward him,
Each of them thinking the other's pain.
The sailor threw his Italian spear
And Byrtnoth was hit; he pushed quickly down   135
With his shield and burst the wooden shaft
To splinters; the spear sprang out. Then,
Angry, he shoved his spear through the guts
Of the proud Dane who'd wounded him. Wise
In war's tricks, he stabbed his javelin   140
Deep in the dangerous Viking's neck,
Reached to his life and let it spill free.
Then he quickly turned on another,
Shattered his mail, threw the poisoned
Point between the woven rings   145
Into his heart. And the earl was happy
And laughed and gave thanks to God for what
The day had granted him.
                        But a Danish hand
Threw a careful spear, ran it far   150
Into Byrtnoth's body, and deep. A boy
Was standing beside him, beardless and new
To war: he ripped the bloody lance
Out of Ethelred's earl and flung it
Back as hard as he could. This   155
Was Wulfmar the younger, Wulfstan's son.
The point went in, and the Norseman who'd wounded
His chief lay quietly across his spear.
Then another seaman came stalking the earl,
His rich bracelets, his rings, his hammered   160
Mail, and the jeweled hilt of his sword.
Byrtnoth unsheathed the brown-edged blade,
Broad and sharp, and struck at the sailor.
But another Norseman knocked his arm
Away, and it hung useless. The yellow-   165
Handled sword fell to the ground:

He would never hold it again, or any
Weapon. The old warrior still
Could speak and he called to his soldiers to fight,
Asked his closest comrades for death   170
In victory. Then his legs could hold him no longer;
He looked up at Heaven:
                    "Lord, I thank You
For all the joy earth has given me.
Now, my Father, I need your grace: 175
Allow my spirit to leave me and come
To You, Prince of Angels, grant
My soul a peaceful journey in
Your protection and keep it safe from the devil's
Spite."   180
            Then the pagan seamen killed him,
And both the warriors who'd stood beside him,
Alfmar and Wulfmar, who stayed close to their chief
In death as in life. And those who lost
Their taste for slaughter began to run.   185
Godric, Odda's son, was the first,
Fleeing from honor as he left the lord
Who'd loaded his arms with presents and rings:
He leaped onto Byrtnoth's horse, sat
In a stolen saddle he'd never deserved,   190
And fled with both his brothers, Godwin
And Godwig, none of them fighting men.
They turned from the battle, scurried to the woods,
Flew to the town, and saved their lives,
They and many more than was right   195
If kindness and gifts had kept in their minds,
The memory of Byrtnoth and the honor he'd shown them.
So Offa had warned him, early that day,
When the army assembled in council: many
Spouted courage and flaming words   200
Who would run and hide when the danger was real.
            So the troops had lost their leader, and the king
His earl; all of Byrtnoth's household
Saw that their lord was dead. Then

His proud followers ran at the Danes,   205
Eager, and fearless, and quick. Every
Heart among them hung on a double
Wish: to lose their life, or avenge
Their lord. And Alfric's son whipped
Them on, Alfwin, young and boldly   210
Shouting:
    "Remember how we boasted,
Sitting on benches and swilling mead•,
Drunk with ambition, dreaming of war:
It's come. Now we'll discover how brave   215
We are. You all should know my name,
Born of a mighty Mercian race;
My old father was Alhelm, an ealdorman•,
Wise, and blessed with worldly goods.
None of my country's people shall taunt me   220
With turning away from this army, running
Back to my home, now that my chief
Has fallen in battle. I know no bitterer
Grief: he was both my kin and my lord."
He went forward, weighing his strokes,   225
Until his blade reached to a Viking's
Life, and the seaman lay on the ground
And was dead. And Alfwin's words hurried
His friends and comrades back to the battle.
    Offa spoke, shaking his ashen   230
Spear:
    "Byrtnoth is slain, and Alfwin
Has said the only words we need
To hear. We all must urge each other
To harry the Danes as long as our hands   235
Can hold our weapons, the hard-bladed sword,
The spear and dagger. Odda's weak-kneed
Son, Godric, has betrayed us all:
Seeing our master's horse, many
Saw Byrtnoth riding in flight, and fled,   240
Scattering the army across the field
And breaking the shield-wall. May he be damned

For routing so many men with his fear!"
      Lofson spoke, raising his linden
Shield: 245
      "I swear not to flee a step
From this field, but go further, avenging my lord
In battle. Nor will the brave warriors
Of Sturmer need to taunt me that now,
Lordless, I let my heart turn coward   250
And pull me home. Only the point
Of a Viking spear shall sweep me away."
And he fought angrily, despising flight.
      Then Dunner spoke, shaking his lance,
A simple peasant, shouting above   255
The din, praying that every warrior
Avenge Byrtnoth:
            "No one can flinch
Or falter, remembering our beloved lord."
And then they charged at the Danes, careless   260
With their lives, and Byrtnoth's followers fought
Savagely, praying only that God
Would grant them revenge and Viking hearts
To pierce.
      And their hostage• lent them his eager   265
Hands, a Northumbrian captive from a fighting
Family, Ashforth, Edglaf's son.
He threw himself into their fight, firing
A steady stream of arrows: some
Were caught by a shield, some killed a Dane,   270
And as long as his arms could stretch a bow
He fought on the English side.
                   And Edward
The Long stood in the vanguard, swearing
Never to give up a foot of the ground   275
On which his better lay. He broke
The seamen's shield-wall, struck them down,
And before he joined his chief fashioned
A vengeance worthy of Byrtnoth's name.
And so did Ethric, the earl's comrade,   280

Swinging a furious sword. And Sibricht's
Brother, and many more, splitting
Danish shields and fighting stubbornly.
Shields crumbled and mail rang
With a terrible song. There Offa slew   285
A Dane, who dropped to the earth, and there
Offa himself fell: war
Quickly cut him down, but not
Before he'd filled the promise he gave
His lord, in the boasts he'd always made,   290
That they should both ride back to Maldon,
Come home unhurt, or lie in a heap
Of corpses, killed by the Danes. He lay
As a soldier should, beside his chief.
     Then shields were smashed as the sailors advanced,   295
Hot with war; a host of Englishmen
Were spitted on their spears. Wistan charged them,
Thurstan's son, and struck three
To the ground before he fell and was still.
They fought hard; no ground and no quarter   300
Were given; warriors dropped, heavy
With wounds, their bodies weary, their souls
At endless rest. And all the while
Oswold and Edwold, two brave brothers,
Called out encouragement, begged their kinsmen   305
And comrades to stand firm in the midst of slaughter
And use their weapons well.
           Then Byrtwold
Spoke, lifting his shield and shaking it;
The old fighter proclaimed a solemn   310
Message:
     "Our minds must be stronger, our hearts
Braver, our courage higher, as our numbers
Shrink. Here they slew our earl.
And he lies in the dust. Whoever longs   315
To run from this field will always regret it.
I'm old. I want no other life.
I only want to lie beside

My lord, near Byrtnoth, who I loved so well."
       And Godric, too, Ethelgar's son,   320
Called them to battle. His spear flew
Like death itself, as he stood in the foremost
Rank and hewed and cut down Danes
Till a sword point reached him, and he died. And this
Was not the Godric who'd run from the fighting   325

Religious Poems

Caedmon's Hymn is reputed to be the first Christian Old English poem. It uses formulaic language, labeling God *ece drihten,* "Eternal Lord" (7). (*Drihten,* from *driht,* "warband," is a standard term for an earthly lord.) *Bede's Death Song* is found in the monk Cuthbert's account of Bede's death. Although the eighth-century monk Bede was a learned author of Latin prose and verse, he was also, according to Cuthbert, *doctus in nostris carminibus,* "learned in our (that is, vernacular) songs" and recited a brief vernacular poem as he lay dying. The poem may have been improvised orally or composed ahead of time.

The most moving of the surviving religious poems are *The Dream of the Rood* and *The Twelve Advent Lyrics. The Dream of the Rood* is a dream vision, the earliest known in any European vernacular. A man dreams that the True Cross narrates to him the events of Christ's Crucifixion. The genre of dream vision was of great importance in the late Middle Ages and included works like *The Romance of the Rose* and Dante Alighieri's *Divine Comedy.* The poem opens with a rhetorical call for attention, beginning, like *Beowulf,* with the exclamation *Hwæt,* "Listen":

Listen! I'll tell the sweetest dream,
That dropped to me from midnight, in the quiet
Time of silence and restful sleep.

(1–3)

The Dream of the Rood evokes the world of secular poetry by referring
to Christ as "the young hero" (39) and to his disciples as loyal retainers
burying their "mighty prince" (69). It also says that "the creation
wept" (55), reminding its modern readers of the Norse god Baldr,
accidentally killed by his brother, who could not return from the
realm of the goddess Hel because the malicious Loki (who had engi-
neered his death) refused to weep for his death. Some of the lines
of *The Dream of the Rood* are carved in runes• on the monumental
eighth-century Ruthwell Cross in Dumfriesshire, indicating that the
poem was known before *The Exeter Book* was copied.

The *Twelve Advent Lyrics* are the first part of a collection of three
poems—*Christ I, Christ II,* and *Christ III*—loosely related around
stories of Christ. The twelve short passages that make up the *Lyrics*
are written in a hymnic tone, all (except the first, whose opening
has been lost) beginning *Eala,* "Oh." The *Lyrics* are based largely on a
series of Latin antiphons, seven of which are the Greater Antiphons
sung during Advent. Of the two other poems, *Christ II* focuses on
the Ascension and *Christ III* on Judgment Day. Because *Christ II*
includes Cynewulf's signature in runes, the entire collection of three
poems was at one time attributed to Cynewulf. There is, however, no
indication that *Christ I* and *Christ III* are by Cynewulf.

In the nineteenth and early twentieth centuries, unsigned poems,
especially those of *The Junius Manuscript,* were attributed to Caedmon
because they are biblical and seem to be similar to the works of Caed-
mon's corpus listed by Bede. *The Junius Manuscript* includes *Genesis,
Exodus, Daniel,* and *Christ and Satan. Genesis* consists of two parts;
the long *Genesis A* is exemplified in this collection by the moving
Abraham and Isaac. Genesis A includes a section of different authorship
known as *Genesis B* and presumably translated into Old English from
Old Saxon. *Genesis B* describes Satan as a Germanic chieftain with his
comitatus•. Its stirring portrayal of the devil and the temptation of
Eve has made generations of readers think of Milton's *Paradise Lost.*
The similarity is doubly tantalizing because Milton knew Franciscus

Junius, who owned the manuscript during Milton's lifetime, leading scholars to wonder whether Milton read *Genesis B*.

The Phoenix is a poem whose first 380 lines are adapted from a late classical Latin work, the *Carmen de Ave Phoenice* by Lactantius (c. 250– c. 340). The remaining 296 lines are an allegorical interpretation of the story. The poet makes excellent use of such Old English poetic techniques as alliteration, rhyme, and assonance to emphasizes key points in the story. We include the first 423 lines of the poem, a radiant description of *neorxnawong*, "paradise" (397), and the phoenix who lives there. The poet's conception of paradise is the absence of precisely the unpleasant aspects of life and nature that are emphasized in the elegies.

CAEDMON'S HYMN

Now sing the glory of God, the King
Of Heaven, our Father's power and His perfect
Labor, the world's conception, worked
In miracles as eternity's Lord made
The beginning. First the heavens were formed as a roof   5
For men, and then the holy Creator,
Eternal Lord and protector of souls,
Shaped our earth, prepared our home,
The almighty Master, our Prince, our God.

BEDE'S DEATH SONG: A PARAPHRASE

For no man thinks
More than he need,
Of where he is going
And what he will meet
At the hands of Heaven's King.   5

THE DREAM OF THE ROOD

Listen! I'll tell the sweetest dream,
That dropped to me from midnight, in the quiet
Time of silence and restful sleep.

I seemed to see a tree of miracles
Rising in the sky, a shining cross   5
Wrapped in light. And all that beacon
Was sheathed in gold; jewels were set
Where it touched the earth, and five studded
The shoulder-span. Angels looked on,
The loveliest things in creation./   10
                 No thief had crowned that gibbet;
Holy spirits watched it, and humble
Men, and all glory under the universe.
     It was a tree of victory/
               and splendor, and I tainted,
Ulcered with sin. And yet I saw it —
Shining with joy, clothed, adorned,   15
Covered with gold, the tree of the Lord
Gloriously wrapped in gleaming stones.
And through the gold I saw the stains
Of its ancient agony when blood spilled out
On its right-hand side. I was troubled and afraid   20
Of the shining sight. Then its garments changed,
And its color; for a moment it was moist with blood,
Dripping and stained; then it shone like silver.
     And so I lay in the darkness/
             a long while, watching
In stricken grief the Savior's tree,   25
Until I suddenly heard it speak.
And these were the words of the holy wood:

   "It was long ago (but I won't forget)
When they came to the forest and cut me down,
Pulled me out of the earth./   30
          Ruthless enemies took me
And made me a mocking show,/
             forced me to hold their thieves.
They swung me up on their shoulders,/
               planted me into a hill,
Set me deep and straight./
         I saw the Lord of the world

Boldly rushing to climb upon me
And I could neither bend, nor break   35
The word of God. I saw the ground
Trembling. I could have crushed them all,
And yet I kept myself erect.
     The young Hero, God/
              Himself, threw off His garments,
Determined and brave. Proud/   40
            in the sight of men He mounted
The meanest gallows, to make/
            men's souls eternally free.
I trembled as His arms went round me./
            And still I could not bend,
Crash to the earth, but had/
            to bear the body of God.
I was reared as a cross. I raised the mighty
King of Heaven and could not bend.   45
They pierced me through with vicious/
            nails. I bear the scars
Of malicious gashes. But I dared/
            not injure any of them.
We were reviled together./
            I was drenched with the blood gushing
From that Hero's side as His holy/
            spirit swept to Heaven.
     Cruel things came to me, there   50
On that hill. I saw the God of Hosts
Stretched on the rack. Clouds rolled
From the darkness to cover over the corpse,
The shining splendor; a livid shadow
Dropped from Heaven. The creation wept,   55
Bewailed His death. Christ was on the cross.
     From distant lands the eager ones came
To the Hero. And I was watching it all;
Wrapped as I was in sorrow/
            I bent to their reaching hands,
Humble with courage. They carried/   60
            away almighty God,

Raised Him out of His torment./
        I was abandoned of men,
Standing bespattered with blood,/
         driven through with spikes.
They set down the weary-limbed God,/
         stood and watched at His head,
Beholding Heaven's King/
      as He lay in a quiet sleep,
Exhausted with hardship and pain./   65
       And they started to carve a sepulcher,
With His slayer watching. They chiseled/
        a tomb of brightest stone
And laid the Lord of victories/
       there. And then they sang
A dirge, miserable in the dusk,/
       and wearily began the journey
Home, leaving their mighty/
       prince. He was left alone.
  Yet after His followers' voices drifted   70
Away, we crosses went on weeping,
Standing in place. The beautiful corpse
Grew cold. Then they cut us
Down. We shuddered with fear, and fell.
They buried us deep in a pit, but the faithful   75
Heard of my fate, and came, and dug me
Out, and adorned me with silver and gold.
   Now can you hear, oh Heaven-blessed man,
How evil men have brought me pain
And sorrow. For now a season has come   80
When the men of all the world, and all creation,
Shall honor and worship me far and wide,
Pray to this symbol. The Son of God
Suffered on me, and made me glorious,
Towering on earth, so that every man   85
Who holds me in awe can be healed at my touch.
I was made to be a bitter punishment,
Loathed by men until I led them

To the road of life, and opened its gates.
Listen! The Father of glory has honored me   90
Past any forest tree, the Lord
Himself—as He honored His mother, Mary,
Made her, loveliest and best of women,
For every man to bow to and worship.
   And now I tell you, oh trusted of men,   95
That you shall reveal this sight, disclose
To the world that this is that glorious wood
On which almighty God has suffered
Agony for mankind's millions of sins
And for Adam's ancient fall. On me   100
He tasted death, and then He rose
As God to save all men with His greatness.
He rose to Heaven. He will hurry here
Again, to seek the souls of this earth,
On the day of doom. As God Himself,   105
The Ruler of Heaven, gathering His angels,
He will judge you all, He alone who can judge,
Opening to every man eternity
Or Hell, as each has earned in this fleeting
Life. No one will stand unafraid   110
Of the word the Lord of the world will pronounce.
And He will ask, there among many, for the man
Who would go to death in the name of God
As Christ knew death on this bitter cross.
They will tremble in terror, and few will try   115
To give an answer to God. But none
Need fear who carries faith in his heart,
The sign of this glorious beacon, for they are given
A power, all through this cross of pain,
That shall carry every soul on earth   120
To live with the Lord for whom they yearn."

   I offered cheerful prayers to that cross,
Bravely, once I found myself
Alone again. My spirit was eager

To start on a journey for which it has suffered 125
Endless longing. My hope in life
Is now that I shall see and reverence
That cross of triumph more than other
Men. All my heart's desire
Reaches for that holy tree and seeks 130
Its hallowed protection. No mighty patrons
Shelter me here; they've melted in shadows,
Gone from the joys of this world,/
                              sought the glorious King
And live in Heaven, now, with Him,
Live in His glory. My longing, through every 135
Day, is for that cross of faith
Which I beheld here on earth
To come and fetch me out of exile
And bring me where exultation is,
Joy in Heaven, where the blessèd of God 140
Sit at His table, where bliss is eternal,
There to place me in the midst of glory,
To grant me eternal gladness with the host
Of the saints. May God befriend me, He
Who once suffered agony here on earth, 145
Ascended the gibbet to ransom our sins.
He broke our bonds and gave us life
And a home in Heaven. And hope was renewed
In bliss for those who'd burned in Hell.
The Son triumphed on that journey to darkness, 150
Smashing Hell's doors. Many men's souls
Rose with Him then, the Ruler of all,
Rising to Heaven and the angels' bliss
And the joy of the saints already enthroned
And dwelling in glory, welcoming almighty 155
God returning to His shining home.

CHRIST I: TWELVE ADVENT LYRICS

The beginning of the first lyric is missing

1.

                 . . . by the King.
You are the stone which, once, the builders
Rejected. How right that this glorious temple
Stand on Your rock, Your hands holding
Its towering walls in place, locking them   5
Together, forever unbreakable, so everyone
On earth able to see may stare,
God, at Your endless glory. Bless
This work of Yours with new wonders,
Now, Lord of victories and of truth,   10
Let it remain, come once more
And repair these crumbling walls, corrupted
To ruin; restore this roof with Your knowing
Touch. Your Father shaped us from clay,
From earth: may the Lord of life rescue   15
This miserable host, preserve us from hardships,
Raise us from fear, as He has done before.

2.

           Oh Ruler, Teacher, righteous Lord
Whose hand unlocks life and the blessèd
Road to Heaven, but withholds that shining   20
Journey from unworthy lives—God,
We call these words to our glorious King,
Who made man and knows his distress:
We beg You not to send fearful
Days to us who sit in this dreary   25
Prison, sadly longing for the sun
That You, Lord of existence, will light
Above us, guarding our souls, surrounding
Our feeble minds with Your glory. Make us
Worthy of salvation, as once we were,   30
Wandering from our eternal home, miserable

Here in this narrow, troubled land.
      Men with truth on their tongues tell
How the Almighty delivered us, deep in sin,
Brought us forth: He chose a virgin,   35
Young and guiltless, for His mother, and grew
In her womb with no man's help, a woman
With Child only for the sake of His coming.
No woman ever equaled her, then
Or now; none knew or deserved the touch   40
Of that silent, holy, secret grace.
But it shone around her and spread, opening
Out ancient mysteries, the Godhead
Of our Maker flashing onto darkened pages
Written with unknown wisdom, the song   45
Of prophets and saints; God came,
And dusty words glowed, desire
For the Lord, and His praise, spoke, and was loud
And was clear; those who had sought Him were heard.

3.
      Oh vision of peace, Holy Jerusalem,   50
Best of cities and birthplace of Christ,
Forever the home of kings, only
In you can the souls of the righteous rest
Exulting in endless glory. Your walls
Stand unstained; sin and evil   55
Shun you, hardship and crime and war
And punishment. You are wonderfully filled with a sacred
Hope, and with joy, according to your name.
Now look around you, across the wide world
And above you, at oceans and the great hanging   60
Arch of the sky—see how Heaven's
King comes to you, longing for His death,
Embracing fate as, long ago,
Prophets' wise words announced, proclaiming
That marvelous birth, declaring, oh noblest   65
Of cities, your consolation and joy.
He has come, took flesh and left it to change

The Jews' pain, and yours, to happiness,
And to break the bonds of sin. And He has known
How the poor and suffering must seek mercy.   70

4.
        "Oh Virgin, even in Heaven all women's
Delight, loveliest of brides, more beautiful
Than anyone heard of or seen on this earth,
Tell us your mystery, explain how the Lord
Sent you His Son, conceived the Child   75
You would carry and bring forth, but loved you differently
Than a husband, never knew you as a wife. Nothing
In this world was ever so wonderfully strange,
No one in history has known grace
So complete, and no one living can hope   80
To share it, as far as the future runs.
Truth and faith and His favor all grew
And flourished in your womb, Heaven's majesty
Dwelled in you, your purity still perfect, immune to
Corruption. Yet the sons of men plant   85
Before they harvest, and then bring forth
In pain and torment." That perfect woman
Answered, Mary, eternally triumphant:
        "Sons and daughters of Jerusalem, what wonder
Is this that amazes your souls and is mourned,   90
Like sorrow and grief, with sighs and moaning?
Why yearn for knowledge of how I remained
A virgin, was no man's bride and bore
God's glorious Son? That secret is meant
For no man's ear. Christ revealed   95
Through me, showed in David's own blood
How Eve's ancient sin was forgiven,
That curse dissolved, and the humbler sex
Brought to glory. Here is hope
And a promise that now God's favor can rest   100
On men and women both—world
Without end of delight, with the angels in Heaven
And the Father of all truth, forever rejoicing."

5.

    Oh Morning Star, brightest of messengers
Sent to this earth, and to men, truest   105
Radiance of the eternal Sun, clear
And glorious beyond all stars, in every
Season glowing with Your own light!
God Himself brought You forth,
God creating God, Heaven's   110
Glory knowing no beginning. Now
God's other creation calls to You, needing You.
Hoping You will hear us, send us Your holy
Light, praying for Your shining truth
To burn where darkness has covered us over,   115
Here in our long night, crouching
In unending blackness, wrapped in our sins,
Enduring the evil shadows of death.
Now, hopeful, we trust in Your healing
Word, brought us from God, Word   120
Which was spoken in the beginning, which came from God
And was itself eternal God, Word
Which turned into sinless flesh, when the Virgin
Bore our salvation. God walked among us
Pure, the Almighty's Son and the Son   125
Of Man the same, came to our misery
And sorrow, and was joy. We thank You, Lord
Of victory, for ever and ever, grateful for
Your grace in taking our flesh for our sake.

6.

    Oh God of the soul and the spirit, how wisely   130
And well You were called Emmanuel, Your Hebrew
Name, spoken first by the angel
At Your birth! Hidden in that name, but unraveled,
Now, was this message: "The Ruler of Heaven
Has come among us, God Himself."   135
The ancient prophets proclaimed Your coming,
King of Kings and purest of priests:
The great Melchizedek, knowing Your glory

And Your might, declared the Almighty's Advent,
Announced that the Giver of Law and of Faith   140
And of Wisdom would appear, here, to those
Who waited and hoped for Him; God's Son
Would descend to earth, as His Father had promised,
Cleanse and purge the world and journey
Down to the devil, travel to Hell   145
And harrow it with His sacred strength. We waited
Patiently, prisoners in our chains, for the Lord's
Coming. Then weak with misery and sorrow
We cried: "Come now, High King of Heaven!
Bring life and salvation to captives bent   150
With weariness, worn almost to death
By bitter tears. Our only hope
Is You, and all the help we can ever
Have. Come to these heartsick slaves
And take us to Heaven with You, be merciful   155
And kind, oh Christ our holy Savior,
King of Glory! Give us your grace,
Take us with You, and keep the damned
From ruling here on earth. Grant us
Joy in Your eternal might, so our praise   160
May rise to Your ears, we whom Your hands
Shaped and moved. Hear us, from high in
Heaven, forever with God our Father!"

7.

    [Mary:] "Oh my Joseph, Jacob's son,
Born of King David's glorious blood,   165
Why break our peace, divide us apart,
Why wither our love?" [Joseph:] "Some sudden thief
Has stolen my name, brought me sorrow
And taunts, insults and bitter words;
You caused them to be spoken, on your account   170
I've been forced to listen, obliged to endure
Silent pain. Sadness pours from
My eyes, and I weep. God could quickly
Cure me, ease my heart and end

My misery. Oh child, virgin, Mary   175
My unripened bride!" [Mary:] "But why weep
And cry so sadly? My eyes see
No sin in you, find no fault in your heart,
Trace no evil stains. You speak
As though crime and wickedness of every sort   180
Ruled you, had filled your soul." [Joseph:] "Your sprouting
Belly has filled me with pain past bearing!
How can I oppose this vicious talk,
Inventing words to answer their anger
And scorn? The world knows I took you   185
From God's bright temple, a virgin bride,
Gladly wed myself to a woman never
Defiled, but now a woman transformed
As though by the devil. Nothing can help me,
Silence or speech. If I told the truth   190
David's daughter would be stoned to death,
Killed for her crime. But covering your sin
Would be harder still: all men shun
A liar and breaker of oaths; he lives
Like a filthy leper." Then the Virgin opened   195
His eyes, brought light to the darkness of his spirit:
          [Mary:] "By God's Own Son, Saviour of us all,
This is the truth: no one has known me,
Taken me to his bed, touched me, no man
In all the world. Almighty God   200
Chose me, sent the angel Gabriel
To my chaste bed and announced His Child.
The angel told holy truths, said Heaven's
Spirit would shine in me, fill me with
Eternal Glory; I would bear God's noble Son,   205
The Beginning of all light. He made me His temple,
Left Joy and Comfort in my womb, so men
Could surrender sadness and abandon pain—
A perfect miracle, and sinless. Thank Him
Forever, God's Great Son, for taking   210
A Virgin's body, for making men's tongues

Call you His father. Only He
Could turn ancient prophecies to truth."

8.

*The "golden doors" of line 250 are a medieval metaphor of Christ's physical
birth, his emergence from Mary's womb*

Oh just and peaceful King of all Kings,
Almighty Christ: before the world   215
And its glories were made You and Your Glorious
Father were One and You were His Child,
Created in His power and His might! No man
Here beneath God's sky can say—
No man among men can hope for such wisdom,   220
Know so much of Your truth—how the Ruler
Of Heaven, before the Beginning, became
His noble Son. We knew, we peoples
Of the earth, shaped and placed here by Holy
Hands, knew and acknowledged that All-Knowing   225
God, Prince of Creation, had parted
Light from darkness, made day and made night;
His power complete, His judgment supreme,
The Lord of Hosts proclaimed His purpose:
        "This shining light shall be joy forever,   230
Glowing eternally on every life
Brought forth by My creatures, generation by generation."
        It was as He said it should be: radiance
Burst forth at His word, gleaming bright
Above the stars, above men, circling   235
In its seasons—but after, not before He'd placed
His Son alongside Himself, shared
His Heavenly throne: the world followed,
Christ led. Lord, Yours is all knowledge,
And His, of how we came here, and why.   240
No mortal mind can hold the secret
Of Your birth, no wit is so keen, no sight
So clear. Then come, King of victories,

Creator of us all, show us Your mercy,
Grant us Your grace! Teach us Your mother's   245
Descent, quench our longing for Your mysteries,
Knowing what miracles are too dark and how deep
Time covers You and Your Father. Christ
Our Saviour, bless the creatures You made
With Your Advent, unlock these golden doors   250
That stood shut, once, closed
Through all the earth's first days; High Lord
Of Heaven, command them to open, come to us,
Seek us Yourself, become one
Of the lowly and the meek. We cry for Your grace!   255
Lord, the wolf of Hell, savage
And dark, has driven Your flock apart,
Scattered it far and wide; souls
You redeemed with Your blood are harried and oppressed
By the devil, herded into bondage, forced   260
Into slavery. Savior, Protector, we beg You,
Pray from the depths of our hearts: help us,
Save us now! Keep Your miserable
Subjects, weary of exile, from the murderer
Of souls, the fiend, keep him from dragging us   265
Down the abyss of Hell. Let us
Ascend, we whom You made, oh Maker
Of everything, to Your Heavenly Kingdom—though the evil
Spirit reaches for our souls, tempts us
With darkness and sin, tries to lead us   270
Away from glory, draw us into endless
Damnation. Save us, Lord, oh Living
God, from all men's enemy; free us,
Shield and Protector, from the flames of Hell.

9.
*See the prefatory note to Lyric 8, just above, for the intended sense of line 307's
"magnificent doorway." Compare lines 301–325 with the Book of Ezekiel,
especially Ezekiel 44:1–2.*

    Oh most sublime of women, purest   275
Wife the world has known or will ever

Know, how rightly our words praise you,
We whose tongues can speak, telling
Your glory and calling your name everywhere,
Rejoicing that the noblest Prince of Heaven   280
Chose you for His bride. And even Christ's
Blessèd servants, the faithful who dwell
With Him, proclaim you, celebrate you, lady,
And our Lord's holy might in making you
Mistress of that Heavenly Host. All worldly   285
Ranks praise you, and prisoners in Hell—
You alone among women, who yearned
So boldly, craved God so well, that you brought Him
Your pure body, offered it without
Sin. No jewel-adorned bride   290
Walked the earth so wonderfully bright,
Presenting a shining sacrifice, offering
Herself to Heaven, her heart as pure
As her body. You alone brought us
God's sacred servant, the angel Gabriel,   295
Hurrying with our Maker's Word, flying
To announce His Son's coming and the majesty
Of that Birth, a divine Child born
Of a Virgin, all men's merciful Savior,
And you, Mary, forever spotless.   300
          We remember, too, ancient words,
Ezekiel's wisdom, a prophet's true
Vision of the Advent, and of you. He felt
His spirit lifted, raised, till he saw
Life and all Eternity. And his knowing   305
Eyes beheld everything, watched
Till they saw a magnificent doorway, its great
Panels decorated with precious gems,
A heavy door wound around
With marvelous bands. And Ezekiel believed,   310
Truly, that no living man could ever
Move such a mighty weight, raise
Such massive bolts, unlock so huge
A gate and open it wide. But the angel

Of God enlightened his soul, and gladdened it,   315
Showed him what his eyes could not see, and said:
        "Listen, Ezekiel. Know that these golden
Gates swing wide for God alone.
In time to come, with His endless might
The Father will pass between them; through   320
This door He will search out your world, and after
His coming it will stand eternally closed,
Locked forever. And only He,
Maker and Preserver of men, could open it
Again, move it with His all-knowing Will."   325
        The prophet's vision has been proven true;
What he saw and the angel said the Lord
Has brought to pass. Mary, that door
Is you, the Almighty traveled to earth
Through you, Christ our Savior, and found you   330
Adorned with goodness, chaste, unique
Among women. And the Father of angels and men,
Giver of life, left you stainless,
Closed your body against sin. Show us,
Now, that glorious gift, sent   335
From Heaven and announced in Gabriel's voice.
Reveal, Virgin, our comfort and joy,
Your Son: let us see Him, and know Him,
Mother of God. Hope has been born
In our hearts, beholding that Child held   340
To your breast; our faith grows and holds firm.
Pray for us, Mary, beg your Son
To lift us free of this valley of death,
To keep us from walking in the ways of sin
And bring us there to His Father's Kingdom,   345
To live forever where no sorrow comes,
In eternal glory with the Hosts of God.

10.

        Oh Holy Lord of Heaven, You
And Your Father lived in that noble place,
Ruled together, before time began.   350

None of the angels existed, then,
None of the mighty Hosts of Heaven
Who guard and keep Your Kingdom, Your glorious
Home and Your Father's, when You worked Your wonders,
You and He, making world   355
And stars and all this great creation.
In You, and in Your Father, rests
The joy of the Holy Ghost. Now
Your creatures join in a humble prayer,
Lord and Savior and God, beg You   360
To hear Your servants' voices. Our souls
Are tormented by our own wild longings.
Here in our miserable exile devils
And damned souls twist their savage
Chains around us. Our only safety   365
Is in You, eternal Lord: help
These sorrowful prisoners of sin, let
Your Coming comfort our misery, despite,
Oh Christ, our bitter lusts and our crimes
Against You. Pardon us, remember our misfortunes,   370
Our stumbling steps, our feeble hearts,
Remember our helplessness. Come, King
Of men, come now, bring us Your love
And Your mercy; deliver our souls, grant us
Salvation, God, so that in all we do,   375
Now and forever, our days on earth
Will work Your holy will among men.

11.

    Oh Heavenly Trinity, radiant in Your perfect
Glory, sublime and holy, worshiped
Everywhere on the broad face of the earth: 380
Now that our Savior has come, revealed
To the world as He'd promised, how rightly we praise You,
Raise our humble voices in reverence
And Your honor, exalt You with all our strength.
And all the seraphim, set in glory,   385
Bold and righteous and quick, eternally

Honor You, there with the angels, pouring out
Song after song in Your praise, their voices
Lovely and clear and strong, their singing
Echoing far and near. Their task   390
Is easy, a service assigned them by our Lord
To allow them the delight of His presence, seeing Him
Eternally near; shining creatures,
They celebrate Christ across His vast Kingdom,
Shielding the Almighty, God Everlasting,   395
With their sweeping wings, crowding eagerly
To His royal throne, leaping and fluttering
About Him, seeking to fly close
To the Savior as He rests in His court of peace.
To exalt their Belovèd, glorify the noble   400
Creator of the universe, they proclaim these bright-tongued
Words:
          "Holy Prince of angels,
Lord of victory and of truth, King of
Kings! Your splendor will glow forever,   405
Honored in all corners of the earth, in every
Time, by all voices. Oh God
Of Hosts, Who filled Heaven and earth
With Your glory, Protector of men, Preserver
Of life, let Your divine exaltation   410
Endure forever; let Your earthly
Praise be forever bright. Blessèd
Christ, who came to us in Your Father's name,
Brought comfort to our misery, may Heaven always
Sing Your glory, praise You without end."   415

12.
          Oh wonderful miracle worked among men,
Our gracious Lord and Maker taking on
Sinless flesh, born from a Virgin's
Body! And she innocent of man's
Love, the Lord of victory growing   420
In her womb through no man's seed, fruit
Sown by mysterious powers no man

Can know: but the Glory of Heaven, God's
Own Son and our Lord, came to His mother's
Body for mankind's sake. And our Savior   425
Was born, great God of Hosts, to offer
Eternal forgiveness; He made Himself a man
To grant men His help. Knowing
His birth we praise Him in our prayers and our lives,
Faithful and eager for His love. A man   430
Whose mind is opened with wisdom sees
How we need to worship our God, honor Him
In our hearts and our speech, always exalt Him.
And the Lord repays love with mercy
And peace, the Holy Savior in Heaven,   435
Allowing the faithful to leave this world
For a new and better one, a land of delight
Where the blessed live forever in eternal
Joy, world without end of bliss.
                          Amen.

GENESIS A: ABRAHAM AND ISAAC

*This episode comprises the final 91 lines of the poem; it is here numbered to
correspond with George Krapp's* Junius Manuscript *edition (Anglo-Saxon
Poetic Records, 1:84–87). Genesis A was once thought to be the work of
Caedmon.*

And then God determined to tempt
Abraham, test His blessèd prince
And try his strength. The Lord's stern voice
Called: 2850
         "Go, Abraham, take
Isaac, your only son, and go
Quickly. Your child must die on my altar,
And you must make the offering. Leave
This place, and climb the steep mountain,
Ringed around with rocky/   2855
                    peaks, which I shall show you.
Ascend on foot, and there/
                    build a funeral fire,

A blazing mound for your son,/
                    and take your sword and kill him
In honor of my name, and let/
                    the dark flames destroy
The flesh of his beloved body,/
                    burn it and leave me my offering."
Abraham hurried to obey, began   2860
To prepare for his journey. The Ruler of angels
Spoke Law, and Abraham loved his Lord.
He rose from his bed, that blessèd prince,
No rebellion in his heart, no protest at his Lord
And Savior's command: quickly, he dressed   2865
And called for his gray sword,/
                    declaring that fear of the King
Of angels still dwelled in his breast,/
                    and filled it. He ordered asses
Saddled, that saintly old giver/
                    of rings, and commanded two men
To ride with him. They were four/
                    in all, his servants, himself,
And Isaac his son. And then he was ready   2870
And left his dwelling, leading his half-grown
Son, exactly as God had said.
He drove the beasts, hurried them down
Winding desert paths, as the Lord
Had declared, until the glowing source   2875
Of day and light rose over the deep
Ocean a third time, and that blessèd
Man saw, as the Prince of Heaven
Had told him, a steep, towering mountain.
      Then Abraham turned to his servants, and said: 2880
"Wait here, my men; both of you stay
At this camp. Isaac and I will return,
Come back down the mountain once we've done
What God, King of our souls, has commanded."
      Then the prince, and Isaac his only son,   2885
Climbed through woods and groves to the place
His Maker had appointed. The boy brought wood,

Abraham brought fire and his sword. As they walked
The child began to ask his father:
      "We've brought fire, my lord, and a sword,   2890
But where is the burnt offering, the sacrifice,
You plan to kill in God's bright name?"
      Abraham answered, never intending
Anything but whatever the Lord commanded:
"The King of Truth, Protector of Men,   2895
Will provide a victim as He thinks it best."
      Then he climbed steadily on, up
The steep mountain, Isaac at his side,
Until he stood at the top of that towering
Place, in the spot the Almighty, Creator   2900
Of covenants and men, had directed. Then he built
The funeral pyre, and kindled flame,
And bound his son, foot and hand,
And lifted the boy and laid him on the pyre,
And swiftly took his sword in his hand,   2905
Ready to kill his son, Isaac,
Pour his blood, smoking and hot,
For the fire to drink. Then God's messenger,
An angel high in the clouds, called
To Abraham with a loud voice. And Abraham   2910
Stood and listened for the angel's words.
And the servant of eternity's Lord, hidden
In Heaven, spoke quickly, saying:
      "Belovèd Abraham, take back your child,
Lift him from the pyre alive, your only   2915
Son! God has granted him glory!
And you, son of a Hebrew father,
Accept your reward from the hands of Heaven's
King Himself—rewards beyond number
For the victory you've won, joy and grace   2920
From the Savior of Souls, to whom you were loyal,
Whose love and protection meant more than your son."
      The fire burned out. God had filled
Abraham's heart with joy, allowing him
Isaac, his only son, alive.   2925

Then Lot's blessèd kinsman, Haran's
Brother, looked suddenly and saw
A ram standing nearby, its horns
Caught in bramble. Abraham took it,
Quickly raised it onto the pyre   2930
In Isaac's place, then killed it with his sword:
Its steaming blood stained the altar
Red, a perfect burnt offering
To God. And Abraham thanked the Lord
For the ram, and for all the blessings, the happiness,   2935
God had sent him, and would send again.

GENESIS B

Lines 235–851 of the Junius Manuscript "Genesis," *here renumbered*

"But enjoy all the rest, you two. Avoid that one tree;
Be careful of its fruit. Whatever you want will be yours."
Then they bowed their heads to the King of Heaven,
Grateful and glad, and thanked Him for His gifts
And all they had learned from His teaching. And God   5
Almighty, their powerful King, gave them
That land to live in, and returned to Heaven.
His creatures remained on earth, with nothing
To complain of, their only task to do
His will forever. And He loved them deeply,   10
As long as they chose to keep His commandments.
        And with His mighty hand, the Ruler
Of Everything, God Almighty, had arranged
His angels in ten ranks, trusting
All would dutifully obey His orders   15
And do His will, their minds and bodies
Created, shaped and endowed by Him.
How glorious He had made them!/
                        And one among them he'd endowed
With so strong and mighty a mind,/
                        and allowed him to wield so much
Power, that he had become/   20
                second in Heaven, so radiant,

So potent and gracious and pleasant/
                with the glory in which God had wrapped him,
That he glowed like stars in the sky./
                    He ought to have loved and honored
His Lord, and delighted in his own/
                  pleasures in Heaven, and been thankful
For the light which God had shared/
                with him: it could have been his
For all eternity./   25
         But he turned to evil and began
Stirring rebellion against/
            Heaven's High Ruler on His throne.
Our Lord loved him dearly,/
              but His angel's flagrant arrogance,
His rebellion against his master, his hateful
Words, his boasting•, could not be hidden
From Him. He refused to serve his God,   30
Saying that he himself shone dazzlingly
Bright: his pride was far too great
To let him continue subservient to God,
A mere servant. It seemed to him
That the angels who belonged to him were stronger   35
And far more skillful than those in the service
Of All-Holy God. He spoke a host
Of boastful words, convinced he could build
A mightier throne than God's, and set it
Still higher in the heavens. He said he meant   40
To begin constructing fortified walls
To the north and west. He seriously doubted
He was likely to remain one of God's servants.
    "Why must I work for Him?"/
                  he said. "I have no need
For a lord and master. My hands make miracles   45
Equally well. I command great power,
I can fashion a wonderfully godlike throne,
Still higher in the heavens. Why must I serve Him,
Drop to my knees before Him?/
               I can be just as godlike as he is.

I have strong fighters behind me,/   50
                           who will not run from battle,
Brave warriors, bold/
                      and heroic, who chose me to become
Their lord and leader. One can plan/
                          and plot, with such noble companions,
And win, with them at your side—/
                       beloved friends, all of them,
Their hearts loyal and firm./
                     I can be their lord and lead them,
I can rule this kingdom. How wrong it would be,   55
Thinking I need to fawn on this God,
Or can get much good from my flattery./
                         I won't serve him much longer!"
       And when God Almighty heard that His angel
Was swollen with pride and stirring up quarrels
With his Holy Lord, speaking rash words   60
Against Him, the angel was obliged to pay,
Accept his share of the pain/
                     and receive his just punishment
For the greatest of all sins, as any man will
Who tries to oppose the Lord on high,
Committing crimes against God./   65
                  And the Lord's heart was angry,
The Almighty high in Heaven,/
                 and He threw him down from his throne.
He'd earned the Lord's hatred,/
                  completely fallen from His favor,
Offended Almighty God./
               He'd fought the Ruler of Heaven
And was forced to descend to earth,/
                 to the horrible pangs of Hell.
Denied God's Holy favor,/   70
              he was thrown down to the deepest
Depths of Hell, and became a devil,
The fiend and all his followers./
                For three nights and days

They fell from the heights of Heaven, angels
Of Heaven descending to Hell,/
                     and God transformed them all
To devils. They refused to honor His word   75
Or His deed, so Almighty God dropped them
Down into darkness, under the earth,
In the blackness of Hell, deprived of their victory.
And every one of the fiends lay
In that slow-moving night, in unending fires,   80
Until at dawn the east wind brought them
Freezing cold. Whether fire or frost,
Some grim affliction was constantly gnawing,
Punishments designed for their pain,/
                        specifically meant for them,
For their world was different, Hell being filled   85
With apostate angels. Only those
Who had honored God were left in Heaven.
      The others, now fiends, lay/
                  in the fire, those who had dared
Oppose their Lord. They suffered torments—
Surging flames in the middle of Hell,   90
Leaping fires and black clouds
Of bitter smoke—because they'd abandoned
Their God's service. Pride had betrayed them,
These arrogant angels, unwilling to honor
The Almighty's word; they were wracked with pain,   95
Fallen to the bottom of the deepest fires
Flaming in Hell; folly and over-
Whelming pride drove them to a different
Land, without any light but full
Of fierce fire. And they understood   100
That all they had won, with their high-flowing boldness
And more than anything else their pride,
Was endless suffering. God was all-mighty.
      Then they listened to their arrogant king,/
                 once the most glittering of angels,
Brightest in Heaven and his Lord's beloved,   105

God's own favorite, till they turned presumptuous
And their wickedness filled the Almighty's heart
With a sudden flood of anger./
                    And down he went into torment,
Flung onto that death-bed./
                  Then God changed his name,
Our Lord in Heaven declared that now   110
He'd be known as Satan, and he'd govern the dark
Blackness of Hell, and not fight with God.
Satan spoke, and his words were sorrowful,
From that day forth the ruler of Hell
And its lord forever. He had been God's angel,   115
Gleaming in Heaven, till ambition seduced him
—But most of all pride, more than anything pride—
And he would not honor the word of God,
The Lord of Hosts. Pride was boiling
Deep in his heart, as horrible torment   120
Surged around him. And these were his words:
      "This tight-bounded place is wholly unlike
That other home we once had, high
In Heaven, which my Lord had granted me,
But wouldn't allow us to keep, neither   125
Our lands nor our power. Still, He was wrong
To throw us deep to the bottom of these fires,
This flaming Hell, and deprive us of Heaven,
Which He has decided, now, to people
With human beings. That pain is the worst—   130
Adam, shaped out of earth, will sit
On that heavenly throne which was mine;
He will live in pleasure, and we will suffer
The pains and torments of Hell./
                  If only I had the use
Of my hands, and could be out of here for a moment,   135
The length of one winter, then with this army—
But here I lie, tied around
And around in iron. I have no power,
Tightly fettered by these hard bands,
These hell-born chains. Above us and below us   140

These fires rage. Never have I seen
A more loathsome landscape. These hellish fires
Never die down. I cannot move:
These cruel, iron-hard rings hold me
Helpless where I am. My feet are chained,   145
My hands are tied. The gates of this Hell
Are locked against us: neither you nor I
Can escape these bonds. These heavy irons,
Hammered on a red-hot forge, have been wound
All around me. God has wrapped   150
These chains around my neck,/
                   showing that He knows my plans,
And also that He knows, the Lord of Hosts,
That Adam would come to harm at my hands,
If I had the use of them, because/
                of those lands in Heaven that were mine.
     Yet now we suffer the pains/   155
              of Hell—the darkness, the heat—
Savage, unending. God Himself
Swept us down to these dark/
            mists. Can He say we have sinned?
That we did Him some palpable harm?/
              Yet He's cut us off from the light,
Thrown us to the worst of all punishments.
We must not withhold our vengeance,
Refrain from doing Him harm/   160
         —He who's deprived us of light.
He's set up a middle-earth/
         and there He's fashioned humans
After His image. He'll use them to people
Heaven with purified souls./
       This must be carefully considered,
In case we're ever able to hurt
Adam and his descendants, pay him   165
Back, keep them all/
      from getting what they want. If we can.
For myself, I no longer believe/
        in that eternal brightness he hopes

To enjoy, with angelic cunning,/
                     for never to the end of time
Can we expect God's mind/
                     to change. Let's steal away
From humans what we cannot have/   170
                     for ourselves; let them lose His favor,
Transgress against His word./
                     Let His anger be aimed at them;
Let them be banished, like us./
                     They'll have to seek out Hell,
These savage, endless depths./
                     And we, too, will have our servants,
Mankind bound with these chains./
                     Let's begin planning our campaign!
If any of my followers had princely gifts   175
From my hands, once, when we lived happy
And blessed in Heaven, in the power of our thrones,
There'd be no better time to return
My favor and pay me back, if anyone
Here has a mind to be helpful and the strength   180
To rise up out of this place and break
Through these gates and walls, and the skill to fly
On his feathered wings and make his way
Through the cloudy sky, and come where those creatures,
Adam and Eve, stand in their earthly   185
Kingdom, in the lap of luxury, while we
Lie here in these depths. God values them
More than us; He may well give them
The riches that we should have, in Heaven,
Which are ours by right. He's set them aside   190
To give to these humans. It hurts me deeply,
Offends my pride, that Heaven will be theirs
For ever and ever. So if any of you
Can arrange for them to forswear the word
Of God, His love will turn to loathing.   195
They'll break His solemn commandments,/
                     And He'll be wild with anger.

And then they'll lose their riches,/
          and He'll prepare some punishment,
Cruel and hard. All of you: think!
How will we trick them? I'll rest easy
In these chains, knowing they've lost that kingdom.   200
Whoever brings that about will earn,
In time to come, whatever rewards
We can win for ourselves, here in these fires.
I'll let him sit at my side,/
          whoever returns to this burning
Hell and tells me that Adam and Eve   205
Have dishonored the teachings of Almighty God,
Disdained His words and His deeds [. . .]"
    An enemy of God, anxious to do battle,
His mind malicious, made himself ready,
Set a helmet on his head which made him/   210
          invisible, and fastened it tightly,
Buckled and clasped it; he was quick with his tongue,
With crooked words. Then he flew up
And (stubborn and determined) passed through the gates,
Floating with the wind, evil in his heart,
Beating away the flames with his fiendish   215
Wings. He meant to deceive humans,
Who were loyal to God, with his wicked words,
Seduce and corrupt them for God to loathe.
And so he journeyed, with his fiend's cunning,
Until, on earth, he found Adam,   220
God's own creation, skillfully fashioned,
Finished and ready, and with him his wife,
A beautiful woman, both of them taught
By God Himself, prepared, ordained
By the Ruler of mankind, the Lord on high.   225
Two trees grew nearby, covered
With clusters of fruit, their branches heavy
With the weight; both were planted by God,
Heaven's High King, with His own hands,
So the sons of men would be able to choose   230

Between good and evil, selecting for themselves
Joy or woe. But the fruit was different,
On one tree delightful, beautiful, shining,
Noble, soft (this was the Tree
Of Life), bringing eternal life   235
On earth to whoever ate of its flesh,
All the evils of old age held off,
And desperate sickness; they would live long,
In happiness and pleasure, and thus pass their days,
Enjoying God's favor here on earth,   240
Honored with the certain knowledge that when
They left this earth, they would travel to Heaven.
But the other was black from top to bottom,
Dark and dry: the Tree of Death,
And it bore bitterness. Eating its fruit   245
Forced on a man knowledge of good
And evil interwound on earth. And forever
After, whoever tasted what grew
On that tree would live in sweat and sorrow.
Old age would steal the deeds he had done,   250
And his pleasures, and his power, and death would snatch him.
For a little while he could savor his life,
And then he'd be sent to the blackness of Hell,
Where he'd serve devils for an endless time —
Man's greatest danger. The devils' loathsome   255
Messenger, God's enemy, knew all this.
          Using his devils' lore,/
                         he turned himself to a snake
And coiled around the Tree of Death,
Where he plucked a fruit, then went where he knew
He would find the creatures God had fashioned.   260
And then, shaping lying words,
The evil one began to ask questions: "What
Might you want from God, Adam? He sent me
Here from Heaven: not long ago
I sat at His very side./   265
               He told me to find you here

And instruct you to eat this fruit,/
                     which will strengthen your body and mind
And much increase your understanding,
And make you faster and far more nimble,
And your whole appearance will glow./
                       And He also said you need
Not worry about wealth. With grace and good cheer   270
You've honored the Lord's word, gratefully
Accomplished the tasks He's set you, and made yourself
Dear to our Heavenly Lord./
                  There in His glorious light,
I heard Him praise you, and speak of your life.
You are to become His messenger, and carry   275
His word from here. The green fields
Of the world stretch far, and God sits highest
Of anyone in the Kingdom of Heaven, Ruler
Of all He looks down on. Coming to you
So far would cause Him, Lord of all men,   280
Too much trouble, so He sent his subordinate—
Me—to tell you. I've been ordered to teach you
Carefully, so follow His instructions
Exactly as He gave them. Take this fruit,
Bite, and eat. Your heart will swell,   285
Your appearance will improve. Almighty God,
Your Master, has sent this assistance from Heaven."
     A man not created by men, Adam
Stood still, and answered: "When I heard the Lord
Of Victories, Almighty God, speak to me   290
Loud and clear, He told me to live here
And obey His commands, and He gave me this bride,
This beautiful woman, and warned me not
To let this Tree of Death deceive me,
Trap me and ruin me, and He said that whoever   295
Descended to such evil, by his own will,
Would dwell in the darkness of Hell. Perhaps
You tell me malicious lies, perhaps
You're truly from Heaven: I don't know. Your words

Completely confuse me, I can't understand   300
Anything you say. But I know what God,
Our faith and our hope, told me when I last
Saw Him: He told me to obey His words
And do as He'd taught me. I've never seen
Any of His angels who look like you,   305
Nor have you shown me any sign
That the Lord, in His grace, has chosen to send
To make me trust you. So I must not listen,
And you might as well go on your way./
                           My belief in Him is firm,
Almighty God in Heaven,/   310
                    who shaped me with His own labor,
Made me with His very own hands./
                              He's able to shower down
Any blessings He likes;/
                    He needs to send no messengers."
          Angry, the devil turned away
And went to where Eve was standing,
And said to that beautiful woman that Adam's   315
Stubbornness would surely harm
Their children's children: "Almighty God
Will be angry, I know it, if I return to Heaven
After this weary journey, and tell Him
With my own mouth you refuse to do   320
What He sent me, on this errand out of the East,
To tell you to do. Adam's answer
Means He's to come Himself, for his messenger
Can't complete his mission;/
                         and that's why Almighty God
Is sure to be angry. But if you, as a faithful   325
Wife, will listen to the words I speak,
Perhaps you can think of some way to obey Him.
Think, deep in your breast,/
                            how you can keep this punishment
Away from you both, as I will explain.
Just eat this fruit! And your eyes will see   330

So far they can find their way around
The world, and farther, even to the throne
Of your Heavenly Master, and He will reward you.
And you'll be able to control Adam,
If he desires you enough/   335
               it will lead him to trust your words.
Tell him truly the wonderful gift
Deep in your breast, because you've done
As God taught you, and he'll give up this struggle,
And wipe away from his heart the ugly
Answer he gave me. Surely, the two   340
Of us can persuade him! Entice him, tempt him,
So he does what you tell him and God will not
Be driven to anger against you both.
Manage that, oh noblest of women,
And I will say nothing to our Lord of the vile   345
Words Adam hurled at me.
He accuses me of lying and wickedness—
Not an angel of God, but a servant of evil.
But I've spent long years under Heaven's high roofs,
And I know the angels well: I've served   350
My Master, our Lord Himself, for years
And years, with great devotion and pure
Good faith. Do you think I look like a devil?"
      And with his tricks and lies he lured her
Into evil; the snake's advice   355
Bubbled in her brain (for our Lord had endowed her
With a weaker mind) until his words
Began to convince her, and against God's orders
She allowed the fiend to give her fruit
From the Tree of Death. No human soul   360
Could have sinned more profoundly! How strange that Eternal
And Almighty God would let so many
Of his servants be led astray because
Of these lies, whispered like seductive truths.
      Then she ate that fruit, against the Almighty's   365
Express prohibition. And the fiend who'd deceived her,

Slyly seduced her, gave her the power
To see far and wide: but it came from him,
Not the fruit. And Heaven and earth glowed
Brighter, and seemed more beautiful, and the work   370
Of God greater, but the sight she saw with
Was no human vision, but a devilish spell
Wound around her soul to trick her
Into thinking she saw. And then the fallen one,
Impelled by evil, not truth (offering   375
Nothing truly worth knowing), told her:
"Now you can see for yourself,/
                              so I need not say a word,
Oh virtuous Eve, that everything's changed,
All things and creatures, now/
                              that you've put your trust in my words,
Followed my advice. Now the bright light   380
I've brought you from Heaven shines and glows
More brightly than before. Now it is yours.
Tell Adam what your eyes can see
And my knowledge has brought you. If he can modestly
Do as I tell him, he too shall enjoy   385
The great fullness of light I've given
You. Nor will I blame him/
                              for his filthy words, which were so
Offensive that he should not be excused."
        Which was how her children would have to live,
Making amends when they'd done something evil,   390
As compensation for their loathsome/
                              acts, so God could forgive them.
        She hurried to Adam, that loveliest woman
Ever to appear on this earth, shaped
By the holy hands of God Himself—
Though deceived by the devil's lies, tricked   395
By his cunning, she'd already secretly broken
The Almighty's laws, done loathsome things
That were bound to make God angry at heart
And cost them His favor, lose them Heaven

For a very long time. Men must carefully   400
Guard their actions, or live to regret them!
    She carried one of the evil apples
In her hand, and one in her heart, God-
Forbidden fruit from the Tree of Death,
For the King of Glory had long since said   405
That his human subjects need not suffer
That greater death; our Holy Lord
Would grant Heaven, and endless happiness,
To each of His people, if only they let
The bitter fruit on the branches of that loathsome   410
Tree hang where it was, untouched—
The Tree of Death, forbidden by God.
Thus he who was hated by God, the King
Of Heaven, seduced Eve's mind with his lies
(Her weaker mind), and she trusted his words,   415
Accepted his counsel, truly believing
The commands he'd so carefully taught her were words
He'd carried down from God in Heaven,
Showing signs and making promises
In great good faith. And she came to Adam,   420
And said: "My lord and master, this fruit
Is wonderfully sweet and good, and this angel
Is God's good messenger, dressed, as my eyes
Assure me, like all the angels of our Lord,
The King of Heaven. How much better for us   425
To win his favor than make him dislike us.
If you spoke harsh words, earlier today,
He's prepared to forgive you, if only we give him
Our willing submission. What good can it do you
To quarrel with your Lord's angel? We need   430
His approval, for he can intercede
With our Almighty Ruler. I can see from here
Where He who made this world is sitting
On high (to the south and east), surrounded
By abundance. I see His angels hovering   435
Around Him on their wings—how many there are,

Dwelling in such joy! How could he give me
Such a gift, unless it were sent by God,
Directly from heaven? And I hear and see
So far and wide, across the whole world,   440
And even beyond, that the sounds of celestial
Happiness reach my ears. My mind
Is enlightened, inside and out, since I ate
This fruit. I have some here, my good lord:
I offer it gladly. I believe it comes   445
From God, at His command; this messenger
Speaks the truth. There's nothing else like it
In all the world—for just as he says,
This angel, it comes directly from God."
      She spoke to him over and over, enticed him   450
All day to commit the dark deed and break
Their Lord's commandment. The loathsome messenger
Lingered, leading them on with desires,
With bright, bold words; having traveled
So long and dangerous a road, the fiend   455
Hung close beside them, resolved to cast
Mankind down in that great death,
Guiding them so astray that they give up
The Almighty's gift, abandon what the Ruler
Of Heaven had offered. Ah! The fiend   460
Was well aware that they'd have to face
The anger of God, and the gates of Hell,
Knew they'd be forced to accept oppression,
Once they'd broken God's commandment,
As he knew that the lying words with which   465
He'd tricked that lovely woman, most beautiful
Of wives, had made her speak with his tongue,
Had turned God's creature, fashioned by His hands,
Into a devil's helper, a tool for deceit.
      And so that loveliest of women talked   470
And talked to Adam, and slowly the man's
Mind changed, and he started to believe
The promises made by his wife's words.
She meant to do good, not evil;/

she had no idea of the host
Of sorrows, the pain that mankind was compelled   475
To endure once she took to heart
The counsel the fiend spoke in her ears.
She thought she'd win the favor of Heaven's
Great King with the words, and signs, and promises
She offered the man, intending to do good,   480
Until the heart in Adam's breast
Turned itself around and did
What the woman wanted. What he got from his wife
Were Hell and death: though no one used
Those words, but said it was only fruit,   485
The fiend had deceived them, it was death's own sleep,
Hell and death and man's damnation,
Mankind's murder—that was the evil
Fruit they ate. And as it entered
Adam, and reached his heart, the bitter   490
Messenger laughed and danced, and happily
Hailed his master: "Surely I've earned
Your favor, now, and filled your heart
With satisfaction. Adam and Eve
Have fallen, and mankind with them. They've broken   495
His laws, refused His commands, and certainly
Lost His favor. They'll never dwell
In His Heavenly kingdom, but fall, instead,
To the darkness of Hell. And you are free
Of at least this sorrow, as you lie there in chains,   500
Knowing you need not worry, in the midst
Of our suffering, the pain of our punishment, deep
In darkness, that men will not live in high Heaven—
Knowing your mighty mind has kept
So many from the pleasures of Heaven's tall towers   505
And beautiful gardens. How angry God was,
The Holy Lord in Heaven, that we
Refused to bow our heads, freely
Submit to His yoke! But it would have been wrong
To live in Heaven merely as His servants.   510
The Almighty's hard and inflexible mind

Was filled with His anger, and He drove us to Hell,
Forced us in immense numbers down
To the flames, toppled our thrones, then set them
Up for men with His own hands,   515
And gave them that kingdom. But let the heart
In your breast be happy, for your will has been done:
Not only have the sons of men surrendered
Their rights to Heaven, consigning themselves
To Hell's hot fires, but God has been hurt,   520
His heart saddened. So whatever/

                          sorrows and torments we suffer,
Adam has paid us back for them all
By earning God's hate and man's damnation,
Inflicting the fear of death./

                     This helps to cure my sorrow;
My heart expands, and is calm;/   525

                 all our injuries are avenged,
The pain we've been forced to endure./

                       Now I'll return where my lord
Lies chained, go back to Satan/

                   bound with iron bands
In the darkness of Hell." And then/

                   that most bitter messenger made his way
Downward, intending to seek the great fires
Burning in Hell, where his master lay,   530
Unable to move. And Adam and Eve
Began to repent, often exchanging
Anxious words, dreading God's anger,
Their Master's fury, and trembling with fear
Of the results it might bring, understanding   535
They'd broken His law. The woman grieved,
Heavy at heart (for it was she who'd abandoned
God's teachings, and His favor), as she watched that light
Fading away, falsely shown her
By the fiend as proof, but had proven only   540
That Hell's pains, and endless disgrace,
Would now be theirs. And their hearts burned
With bitter sorrow. At times they fell

To their knees, praying together, calling on
The Lord of victories, God Almighty,   545
The Ruler of Heaven, begging Him
To let them have their well-earned punishment,
Which they would not protest, for they knew they had broken
His holy laws. And they knew themselves naked,
Their bodies unclothed. They'd lived in no permanent   550
Place, there in that land, nor known
The sorrows of labor; they could have continued
That easy life, if only they'd gone on
Observing God's orders. Husband and wife
Exchanged a host of sorrowful words.   555
      And Adam said to Eve: "Ah!
This evil thing you've done has marked out
Both our paths. Can you see that black Hell,
Eager to swallow us? Listen: you can hear it
Roaring, even from here. Those fires   560
Don't burn in Heaven, the best of all lands,
Which with God's good grace we could have had,
If only you hadn't let the devil
Lead us to break our kind Lord's word,
The King of Heaven. On this account   565
We will suffer and mourn. For He Himself
Warned us both to be on our guard
For this worst of all evils. Hunger and thirst,
Unknown to either of us, from the start
Of time, are tearing bitterly at my breast.   570
How will we stay alive,/
                go on living in this land,
If winds come, from the west or the east,
The south or the north? The world will grow dark,
Hail will shower down from the sky,
And the ground will freeze and be horribly cold.   575
Sometimes the sun will glare down,
Blazing hot, and we'll stand here naked,
With no clothes to protect us. Nothing will shield us,
Whenever it storms, nothing on earth
Will bring us food, now that Almighty   580

God is angry. What will become of us?
And now I regret asking God,
Our righteous Ruler, to create you for me,
From my own limbs, for you've led me astray,
And my Lord hates me. To the end of time   585
My heart will be sorry I ever saw you."
    And Eve answered, most beautiful of women,
Loveliest of all wives; though the devil's cunning
Had seduced her, she'd been shaped by God's own hands:
    "You have the right to blame me with these words,   590
Adam, my friend, and yet it can't
Press harder on you, in your mind,/
                    than it does on me, in my heart."
    Then Adam spoke to her again:
"If only I knew what punishment
The Lord Almighty means to send me: 595
No one could obey Him more quickly, though His hate
Command me to leave this place and sail
Out on the waves, the endless ocean,
No matter how deep. My heart would not doubt Him
Though He sent me straight to the bottom, as long   600
As that was His will. No worldly service
Can ever please me again, now
That I've lost my Lord's favor forever.
But we cannot stay here, we two together,
Naked as we are. Let's hide ourselves   605
In the shadows of this wood." So they turned and left,
Walking into the greenwood, where they sat,
But not together, waiting to learn
God's will, well aware that they could not
Keep the things He'd given them, the Almighty   610
King. They covered their bodies with leaves
And twigs, having no clothing to wear,
But every morning fell on their knees,
Both together, and prayed to God
Almighty not to forget them, begging   615
The righteous Ruler of Heaven to tell them
How they must live out in the light.

THE PHOENIX

Lines 1–423 of a 677-line poem

Far off, at the eastern tip of the world,
Lies a noble land, well known to me
As to every man, but a corner of earth,
Which few men see or come to since God's
All-powerful might expelled us as evil-   5
Doers, turned us out of Eden.
It spreads into beautiful fields, full
Of pleasure and steeped in the loveliest fragrance
On earth, rich and rare like its Maker,
Who set it magnificently into place.   10
When Heaven's doors swing out for the blessed
Their glorious voices ring echoes here.
The gentle plain rolls to a distant
Horizon green with forests, and neither
Rain or snow, nor the blast of frost,   15
Nor blazing fire, nor hail falling,
Nor the sun's glow, nor cold or warmth
Or winter showers can injure anything
Where everything lies securely suspended
In unharmed bliss. All that land   20
Bursts into blossoms. There are no hills,
No mountains, no rocky cliffs towering
Steeply, as there are for us, no sliding
Ravines or valleys, no mountain caves,
No mounds, no ridges, nothing rising or falling   25
Nor anything rough in that excellent place
Where pleasures blossom and grow. And that radiant
Land, the ancient sources of wisdom
Say, reaches twelve times higher
Toward Heaven's stars than any hill   30
That here with us juts brightly, hugely,
Up in the sky. That plain is calm
With triumph, gleaming with sun-filled groves
And pleasant woods where no fruit falls,
No branches wither and trees stand green   35

Eternally, obeying God, hung
With fruit in winter and summer alike.
No colors fade, no leaves decay,
No fires char that beauty nor ever
Can until the world is changed   40
And ended. And when the waters roared
Around the earth, the flood covered
And circled the globe, this noble land
Stood untouched, protected against
The savage waves, blessed, uninjured,   45
Through the favor and grace of God. So
Will it flourish and stay until the fire
Of the Judgment Day when the dead will rise
And their graves stand wide, gaping and dark.
    No enemies walk that land, no weeping   50
Is heard, no signs of misery, no hate,
And neither old age nor crime, nor the clutch
Of death, nor any misfortune, nor feuds
Nor sin, nor struggles or vengeance or troubles,
Nor poverty's anguish or lack of abundance,   55
Nor sleep, nor sorrow, nor sudden illness,
Nor the falling snows of winter or any
Roughness of weather, biting frost
Or gleaming icicles, strike at anyone.
The wind drives no clouds to that land,   60
Drops no hail or frost or sheets
Of storm-blown rain, for there the streams
Are lovely miracles, surging springs
Bursting out to moisten the soil
With sparkling water from the heart of the wood.   65
Like a glorious ritual once a month
The green earth gushes icy streams
Across the groves, pouring, at God's
Command, a flood of splendid rivers
Over all the land. Those woods   70
Are lined with bending branches dipping down
Perfect fruit, and nothing pales
Or lessens in that beautiful, holy spot.

No dusk-red, autumn blossoms drift
To the ground, stripping loveliness out of 75
Wonderful trees, but the heavy boughs
Blossom eternally ripe, always
Green and fresh, exultant ornaments
Dotted upon that brightest plain
By Holy Hands. Nothing breaks 80
The shape of beauty where the immortal fragrance
Hangs over the land. And so it will stand
As in the beginning He made it, enduring until
The end of time and this earth. And all
That loveliness surrounds a single, beautiful 85
Bird, watching over the wood
And his home with strong-feathered wings. His name
Is Phoenix. Death can never follow him
Into that happy land for as long
As the world spins round. In the morning, there, 90
They say he faces the east and the coming
Sun, peering with eager eyes
At the sea gleaming with the shining brightness
Of God's eternal, jewel-like candle,
The noblest star of all swinging 95
Slowly aloft, a radiant emblem
Of our Father's ancient work. The glittering
Stars are swallowed in the swelling motion
Of waves rolling out of the west,
Quenched by the dawn as darkness is snuffed 100
Into vanishing night. And then the noble
Phoenix stares over the water to where
The lamp of Heaven glides out of the sea.
    This is the Phoenix's life, beside
The fountain of bubbling streams, to bathe 105
In the morning twilight, twelve times plunging,
Twelve times tasting the icy water
Welling up from the clear, refreshing
Spring. And after that ravishing delight
He spreads his shining feathers and sweeps 110
Exultant to a towering tree, from where

He can watch and worship at his ease, following
Heaven's taper aglow in the east
And soaring lustrous and sparkling across
God's sky. And all the world glows   115
With that wonderful light, gleaming, adorned,
When the golden gem of the firmament pours
Its splendor over another glorious
Day on earth. And when dawn is day
And the sun has floated up from the salty   120
East, the brightest of tawny birds
Flies up from the grove and with flashing wings
Hurries swiftly into the sky, beautifully
Singing and caroling to Heaven, clamorous
With the passionate joy flooding his heart   125
And impelling him toward God. He rings
The most impassioned variations
With his shining voice that the sons of men
Have heard under any sky since the Lord
And Maker of everything created the world   130
And Heaven above it. The notes of his song
Are sweeter, more gracious, than any music,
More melting than any mortal sounds.
The tumult of trumpets cannot compare,
Nor horns, nor the long-stringed harp•, nor the voices   135
Of any living men, nor organs,
Nor swelling choral harmonies, nor any
Of the pleasures God placed in this murmuring world
For men to delight in. And so he sings
And pours out melodies flowing with bliss,   140
Until the sun dips to the south
Of the sky. Then he is silent and listens,
Quickly nodding his head, confident,
Bold, knowing, shaking his swift-feathered
Wings three times and no more. Then silence.   145
He always marks the hours of every
Day and every night. And this
Is his God-given life, to dwell in the wood
And taste the pleasures of that land, savor

Its treasures of riches and grace, until   150
A thousand winters• enfold the glorious
Sentinel of Paradise. Then the ancient,
Gray-plumaged bird, heavy with years,
Flies out of the green-blowing land, the blooming
Eden, spreads his beautiful wings   155
And searches out a broad and empty
Kingdom where no man has a home
And no man comes. There the most perfect
Of birds meets with his kind and is made
Their king, and there he lives among them   160
A time. But soon, oppressed with years,
He unfolds his swift-moving wings, following
Waves rolling to the west. The birds
Crowd around him, each of them anxious
To serve and honor their greatest glory,   165
And they seek the deserts of Syria in a swarming
Flock. Suddenly, there he flees them,
Seeking shelter for innocence in a grove
In that western place, wrapping himself
In concealment, safe from the eyes of men.   170
And there he finds a firm-rooted tree,
Known by his name, and takes his home
And lives, high among the leaves
And branches of that desert wood. And I know
That tree sprouted from seeds shaped   175
By the glory of God, and grew the tallest,
The broadest and noblest of any set
On our earth; and God granted it eternal
Protection from every evil, shielded it
Forever from any injury. Then,   180
As the wind is calmed and the weather fair
And the sky sparkles with holy brightness
And the clouds are dispersed and the ocean's might
Is at rest and storms and winds are soothed
And quiet, and men bask in the warmth   185
Beaming down from the south, the Phoenix
Begins to build his nest among

The boughs, passionate with longing to quickly
Travel back through time, to find,
At the end of old age, youth and a new life   190
Waiting.
      He gathers, far and near,
The sweetest-smelling herbs and roots,
Collects the loveliest leaves and twigs
And green-barked shoots which the King of Glory,   195
Father of beginnings and creatures and time,
Created on earth in honor of the men
He had made and the world he had made their home.
He bears them himself, brings the treasures
Of earth into the tree and with   200
That splendor shapes a beautiful nest,
High at the top, alone above
The wilderness. Then he withdraws inside
And lines the leafy shade around him
With the noblest, holiest fragrance of fruits   205
And blossoms, completely surrounding his body
And gray-feathered wings. There he stays,
Eager to start. The summer sun,
Lit and burning and busily working
The will of fate, glows on the shadows,   210
Looks down on the world and out of a cloudless
Sky warms the Phoenix's nest.
The herbs, gently heated, give off
Their sweetest scents, and then they burn
And fire seizes the Phoenix and its nest.   215
    It burns.
          Flames are wrapped around it,
Blazing fiercely, pale yellow flames
Feeding on his body and eating away
His covering of years. And then it's gone,   220
Flesh and bone burned in the flames
Of a funeral pyre. Yet in time
He returns, his life reborn after
The flames drop lower and his ashes begin
To fuse together in a shriveled ball,   225

After that brightest nest is burned
To powder and that broken body, that valiant
Corpse, slowly starts to cool.
The fire flickers out. The funeral
Pyre sprouts a rounded apple   230
Out of a bed of ashes, and that pellet
Sprouts a wondrous worm, as splendid
As though hatched from a lustrous, pale-shelled egg.
He grows, flourishing in the holy shade
And soon the size of an eaglet, soon   235
Fattening on pleasure, as large in form
As any proud-winged eagle. Then
His feathers return and he is as he was
At the beginning, blossomed brightly to life
And eternal beauty. His flesh returns,   240
Renewed, reborn, and freed of sin,
As men gather in the fruits
Of the earth, bring home a welcome harvest
When the fields are ripe for reaping, a step
Ahead of winter, watching the sky   245
For clouds and rain that can pour down ruin.
That joyous harvest is food and drink
Against the frost and snow that sweep
The earth and cover it over like an icy,
White-waved flood. And that store of fruits   250
Is the soil of all happiness, all riches, working
Through the simple seeds of grain
Dropped in furrows. In spring the sun
Brightens the sky, the sign of life
Wakes the world, and then the fields   255
Wave with the richness of crops thrown up,
Each according to its kind and its seeds.
So the Phoenix grows, dropping a thousand
Years and taking on youth. Yet he neither
Eats nor drinks, except the drops   260
Of honey dew that fall at midnight,
And this is nourishment enough
To feed him nobly and send him seeking

His home in ancient Eden. And when
The exultant-feathered bird rises   265
Out of herbs and ashes, young
And graceful and graced by God, he gathers
The bits of his body out of the dust
And rubble that the fire has left, skillfully
Assembles the blackened bones and puts   270
Cinders and ashes together, covering
The refuse of the funeral heap with roots
And wonderful blossoms until it wears
The glow of beauty. And then, eager
To travel back to his home, he takes   275
What the embers have charred and left, lifts it
In his claws, and flies toward that perfect place,
His sun-drenched native land, spreading
Wings rejuvenated in glory, wrapped
In all the loveliness that God created   280
For him when setting him down on that shining
Plain. And carrying his burden of bones
And ashes, cleaned and consumed by surging,
Encircling flames, he finds the island
And fills a hole with all that his former   285
Self now is, a strong-winged warrior
Burying himself. And there he sees
The sun reborn, the brightest of jewels
And noblest of stars sweeping over
The ocean and gleaming out of the east.   290
The Phoenix's breast is a flickering rainbow
Of color, bright and beautiful. The back
Of his head is green, delicately, wonderfully
Mixed with purple, and his tail is spread
In lovely divergence, some parts brown,   295
Some purple, some incredibly spattered
With shining spots. His wings whiten
At the tip, his neck is green below
And above, his beak gleams as though set
With glass or jewels, and his jaws shine   300
Inside and out. His eyes are strong

And glow gloriously bright as gems
Held by some wondrous art in sheets
Of thinly hammered gold. A garland
Of feathers flares around his neck   305
Like a ring around the sun. His stomach
Is brilliant and bright, nobly worked.
His shoulders and all his upper back
Are feathers; scales cover his legs
And his red-yellow feet. This is a bird   310
Unlike all others, or like the thousand-eyed
Peacock that scholars describe, growing
And strutting through an aura of color and delight.
Nor is the Phoenix slow, or sluggish,
Or dull and heavy like the birds that heave   315
Their slothful wings through thickening air,
But active and quick, as graceful and light
As he is beautiful to see. For he takes his happiness
From the palms of eternity's prince. So
He sets out again, seeking Eden   320
And his home. And when he passes over
The earth on outstretched wings, people
Appear, run out of their homes, run
From north and south, crowds throng
From every direction, near and far,   325
Collect in a huge assembly to stand
And stare up at the grace of God flying
By in the shining bird, a grace
Fixed in Creation by the King of Truth,
A treasure no other bird boasts. They stand   330
And they wonder at the lovely shape and form,
They inscribe it in books, cut its image
In marble, and keep the day and the hour
When multitudes gathered, and men saw the glory
Of the Phoenix. And as he flies birds   335
Appear, filling the sky, pressing,
Crowding from beyond the horizon and calling,
Shaking the clouds with singing his praise,
Swarming over and under and all

Around him as he moves, the holy one, through the middle   340
Of the turning, milling mass. And men,
Struck dumb with wonder, watch their ecstasy
As flock after flock worship the Phoenix,
Proclaiming his powers, again their king,
Their belovèd leader. And in that delight   345
They lead him toward home until he leaves them
On wings so swift that he flies alone,
Leaving the circling birds and staring
Men and seeking his distant home.
     So the blessèd one survives his death   350
And goes back to the shining land that was his
In a former life. The host of birds
Turn sadly away to other homes,
Reluctant to leave. And then the noble
Creature is young. Only the King   355
Of Heaven, God Almighty, knows it
For male or female, for knowledge of the ancient
Decree that shaped the wonderful bird
And gave it cause and being is kept
For the Maker and kept hidden forever from men.   360
There the Phoenix takes pleasure in the earth
And the running streams and the woods of Eden,
Lying there until a thousand winters
Have fallen and melted and life comes
To an end for him, wrapped in the flames of the funeral   365
Pyre. Yet life is always wonderfully
Awakened, stirred back from bones and ashes.
He is not afraid of sinking to death
With pain and fear, for he never forgets
That for him the flames cool into life,   370
Destruction breeds living and flesh grows quickly
Out of embers, has and always
Will, and in the shade of Heaven
His life begins again. He is both
His son and his father, the eternal heir   375
Of his body and all his ancient estate•.
This was the Almighty's grant at the beginning,

That though fire should carry him off he should be
Forever as he was, clothed in gleaming
Feathers, eternally the same. So is it   380
With each of the blessed, bearing misery
And choosing the darkness of death for themselves
In order to find eternal life
And the protection of God repaying pain
On earth with endless glory and endless   385
Joy. For the Phoenix is very like
The chosen servants of Christ, who show
The world and its towns what comfort and pleasure
Descends from our Father's solace, and how,
In this dangerous time, they can take His grace   390
As a certain sign of lofty glory
To be lived in that celestial land above.
We have learned that the Lord formed men and women
With His infinite power, and placed them, then,
In the most wonderful corner of the world, called   395
Eden and Paradise, where bliss was abundant
And would never fail while mankind kept
The letter of the Word, keeping delight
As long as God was obeyed. But
The arch-fiend's hatred followed them, and his envy   400
Poisoned them, suggested forbidden fruit
And coaxed them down a foolish path
Leading away from God to the taste
Of an apple. They bit, and the fruit was bitter
In their mouths and misery to all their children,   405
A mournful banquet for their unborn daughters
And sons. Their greedy teeth were painfully
Punished.* They angered God and paid
A terrible price, and their children paid
In affliction for Adam's taste of a bit   410
Of forbidden food. And the adder's rancor
Drove them sadly out of Eden,
Seduced the ancestors of us all, in that ancient

*The text is corrupt and uncertain at this point.

Time, with his infinite evil forcing them
Out of their joyous home to the misery   415
Of this valley of death and a dwelling built
In sorrow and tears. Their shining homeland
Was hidden in darkness, and those holy fields
Hedged round by Satan's deceit and treachery,
Shut for centuries till the King of Glory   420
Descended and readied Eden to receive
His saints, and our Joy, our Comfort and only
Hope, restored Heaven on earth.

Wisdom Poetry

This grouping of Old English wisdom poetry is a miscellaneous collection of works whose teaching is partly Christian, partly secular. It consists of riddles, succinct formulations of traditional wisdom, bestiary poems, and metrical charms.

As *The New Princeton Encyclopedia of Poetry* states, riddles are "an ancient and worldwide form in both oral literature and written literature."* The earliest known compilation of riddles in England is found in *The Exeter Book.* This collection consists of one five-line riddle in Latin and some ninety to ninety-five riddles in English (the number depends on how the riddles are divided; for example, the material translated here as Riddles 1, 2, and 3 is sometimes treated as one riddle). Like all the poems in *The Exeter Book,* these riddles are somewhat damaged by knife strokes, liquid stains, and burns; the conclusion of Riddle 87, for example, has been damaged. Like most Old English poetry, these riddles are anonymous, and their date of composition cannot be determined. Because the brief Latin riddle in the collection twice refers to *lupus,* or wolf, the riddles were at one time attributed to Cynewulf, whose name means "the Royal Wolf."

---

*Alex Preminger and T. V. F. Brogan, eds., *The New Princeton Encyclopedia of Poetry* (Princeton, N.J.: Princeton University Press, 1993), 1070.

Although the Germanic tribes who invaded England probably
brought an oral tradition of riddling with them and that tradi-
tion very likely continued, some critics have noted the absence of
references to riddling in such works as *Beowulf* or "The Fortunes
of Men." Because some of the riddles in *The Exeter Book* have Latin
sources—Riddle 40, "Creation," for example, is a translation of Riddle
100, "De Creatura," by Bishop Aldhelm (died 709)—some critics see
the sources of the entire collection as lying in the Latin tradition.
Part of the learned Latin heritage that the Anglo-Saxons had access
to consisted of literary riddles like those of the poet Symphosius
(an unknown writer of about the fifth century), a form practiced by
such writers of the early Christian church as the bishop and historian
Eusebius (265–339?). Latin riddles were popular in eighth-century
England, and some critics believe that the vernacular riddles of *The
Exeter Book* date from the same period.

The case is far from closed, however. The riddles may be of later
composition, and they often differ substantially from those in Latin.
Latin riddles have titles that give the solutions, so that they seem to
be merely exercises in metaphor. The Old English riddles, in contrast,
are literary games. The Old English riddles demonstrate what W. P.
Ker calls "imaginative thought"; "the riddle becomes a shifting vision
of all the different aspects in which the creature may be found—a
quick, clear-sighted, interested poem."* The creatures and objects
speak in their own voices, and the riddles often end as does Riddle 8,
"Who can I be?" (8). In some, the subject of the riddle describes
itself in human terms, as in Riddle 11, in which Wine begins, "I
wear gray." In others, the speaker is a human being describing the
mysterious identity of the riddle's subject; Riddle 29 begins, "I saw
a silvery creature scurrying / Home." Some riddles have an obvious
solution, while others are so obliquely allusive that their solution
is problematic. Most intriguing are the so-called obscene riddles,
which have a straightforward meaning like "key" (Riddle 44). In true
riddling fashion, however, these riddles suggest another meaning
that is not expressed, a witty reference to sexual matters. Proposed

---

*W. P. Ker, *The Dark Ages* (New York: Scribner's, 1904; rpt. London: Nelson,
1955), 92.

solutions for all the riddles presented here can be found at the back of the book.

The pagan• Anglo-Saxons considered *wyrd,* "fate," to be the force that governed human existence, and in Christian times the concept became merged with that of God's Providence. There are many gnomic•, or aphoristic, passages in such Old English poems as *Beowulf,* and there are two extant compilations of wise sayings, known as *Maxims I* and *Maxims II. Maxims I* contains not only gnomic sayings but narrative passages, including a very beautiful description of a Frisian wife welcoming her returning husband, and is translated here. *The Fortunes of Men* is concerned with the paths human beings follow in the world. It includes theological musings about the ways that "Almighty God parcels / Out men's lives across the earth" (64–65) and merges them with popular wisdom:

> Some, swilling ale, and angry,
> Soaked in wine, will meet death
> At the edge of a sword, for their hasty words.

> (48–50)

The poem depicts vividly both the tragic destinies of humankind and the talents given by God to human beings.

Examples of the medieval genre of the "Bestiary" (also known as the *Physiologus*) are found in Latin and in most European languages. Bestiaries describe the traits and behavior of birds and animals, many of them mythological, and the genre is explicitly allegorical rather than based in natural history. Although Continental versions of the *Physiologus* sometimes contain fifty stories, the Old English version consists of seventy-four lines about the panther and eighty-nine about the whale, as well as sixteen fragmentary lines about a bird traditionally identified as the partridge. *The Panther* allegorizes the panther as Christ in combat with Satan, while *The Whale* allegorizes the marine beast as the devil, luring the unwary to damnation. These explicit allegories, which seem to be translated from a Latin original, provide a striking contrast to the elegiac and heroic• poetry.

Embedded in extant tenth- and eleventh-century manuscripts are twelve metrical charms. These short incantations were meant to mitigate against or prevent such natural or legal problems as barren

land, the growth of a wen, and the theft of cattle. The charms are
irregular in meter and do not always employ the four-stress Old
English poetic line; they have little literary merit. The translation
here of a portion of the *Charm for Bewitched Land* shows the practical
nature of the charms: "Soil, be well again" (1).

RIDDLE 1

How many men are so knowing, so wise,
That their tongues can tell Who drives me into exile,
Swells me brave and strong and fierce,
Sends me roaring across the earth,
Wild and cruel, burning men's homes,   5
Wrecking their palaces? Smoke leaps up,
Gray like a wolf, and all the world
Crackles with the sounds of pain and death.
When I shake forests, uproot peaceful
Groves, clouds cover me; exalted   10
Powers hurl me far and wide.
What once protected the world, sheltered
Men, I bear on my back, bodies
And souls whirled in the mist. Where
Am I swallowed down, and what is my name?   15

RIDDLE 2

Sometimes I travel along under
The waves, where no one can see me, hunting
The bottom of the ocean. The sea whips
And heaves, tossing up whitened foam,
Roaring and shrieking. Flooding water   5
Crashes and beats on the shore, hurling
Stones and sand and seaweed and great breaking
Waves on the high cliffs, while I
Go struggling deep in the ocean, thrashing
In its darkness. But I can't escape, pull off   10
The waves from my back, till He allows me,
He Who always guides me. Say,

Wise man, Who draws me from the ocean's arms
When the waters are still again, when the waves
That covered me over are gentle and calm.   15

RIDDLE 3

*This may be a continuation of Riddle 2; Riddles 1–3 may also be parts of one
larger poem*

Sometimes my Master chains me down,
Drives me deep inside the earth
And makes me lie there — my mighty Lord
Forcing me to hide in a narrow hole,
Dark and small, where the world scrapes at   5
My back and I can barely move.
Escape is impossible. And yet I can shake houses
And cities, mead-halls• and palaces, till their walls
Tremble, till roofs and ceilings totter
And heave. The air may hang, gentle   10
And still, the sea may seem calm,
And then I come bursting out of the ground,
Obeying Him Who began the world
And my bondage, Who leads and guides me; He ties me
Tightly to His will, holds me in His hand,   15
Keeps me on His paths, His power complete.
Sometimes I stir up the ocean, swooping
Down, till flint-gray waves fight for
The shore, whipped into foam, struggling
High on the cliffs; hills rear up,   20
Dark; one after another black waves
Break, whirling water rising
And falling, smashing together on the low
Shore below the rocks; ships
Echo with sailors' cries; and towering   25
Cliffs, sloping toward the sea, stand
Unmoved at the edge of wild waves
Smashing on silent stone. Crowded
Boats, caught in that savage season,

Can look for fierce battles, swept   30
From their helmsman's hands, lifted and rolled
On the sea's spiny back, pulled
And beaten to death. This is one of the horrors
I bring to men, obediently crashing
On my rough way. And Who can calm me?   35
      Sometimes I rush through the dark clouds
That ride on my back, breaking the sea
Apart; sometimes I let it slip
Quietly into place. I roar loudest,
Bellow and scream from above cities   40
And towns, when clouds crash their sharp
Edges, dark monsters colliding
As they hurl through the air, spitting shining
Flames; the heavy rumble flares
And surges through the sky, growling, and men   45
Shiver. Black, rustling sheets
Of water pour from these monsters' bellies
And flow on the ground. This whole vast legion
Of misshapen soldiers fills men with fear,
Cowering in their homes as stalking specters   50
Crowd through the air, shooting glittering
Arrows, throwing terrible weapons
At the earth. Only the ignorant stand
Where those death-spears fall, but if God sends them
A flying arrow, aims at their hearts   55
From the center of the roaring whirlwind, and the rain,
They go to their graves: who can escape
When the running rain-spear tracks him down?
      I start that warfare, leaping up
Where the clouds battle, flying across   60
Their crashing field, pushing easily
Over the waves. Noises crack
And echo in the air. And then I sink
To the ground, hidden in the darkness, and gather
What my Lord and Master orders me to steal,   65
Confirmed and renewed in my strength. Thus,
A mighty servant, I wage His wars,

Sometimes buried in the earth, sometimes
Dropping deep through the waves, whipping
The ocean about, sometimes climbing   70
To make the clouds, always swift
And fierce as I travel on His errands. Tell
My name, and Who commands my fury,
And Who can hold me silent and still.

RIDDLE 7

My clothes are silent as I walk the earth
Or stir the waters. Sometimes that which
Makes me beautiful raises me high
Above men's heads, and powerful clouds
Hold me, carry me far and wide.   5
The loveliness spread on my back rustles
And sings, bright, clear songs,
And loud, whenever I leave lakes
And earth, floating in the air like a spirit.

RIDDLE 8

My mouth talks with a thousand tongues;
I sing with an easy art, often
Altering my voice as it rings the loud
Clamor of my song. As an old poet
Of the evening I tune my sliding music   5
Where, in their towns, men take pleasure
In the sound, sitting quietly, sinking
Along my words. Who can I be,
Aping a singing buffoon with a shining,
Brassy voice that bellows happiness,   10
The welcome sound of my strident cry?

RIDDLE 11

I wear gray, woven over
With bright and gleaming gems. I bring

The stupid to folly's paths, fool
The ignorant with sin, urge all useless
Roads and ruin the rest. I can't   5
Explain their madness, for I push them to error
And pick their brains, yet they praise me more
For each seduction. Their dullness will be sorrow
When they lead their souls on high, unless
They learn to walk wisely, and without my help.   10

RIDDLE 14

I was a warrior's weapon, once.
Now striplings have woven silver wires,
And gold, around me. Men have kissed me,
And I've called a field of laughing comrades
To war and death. I've crossed borders   5
On galloping steeds, and crossed the shining
Water, riding a ship. I've been filled
To the depth of my heart by girls with glittering
Bracelets, and I've lain along the bare
Cold planks, headless, plucked and worn.   10
They've hung me high on a wall, bright
With jewels and beautiful, and left me to watch
Their warriors drinking. Mounted troops
Have carried me out and opened my breast
To the swelling wind of some soldier's lips.   15
My voice has invited princes to feasts
Of wine, and has sung in the night to save
What savage thieves have stolen, driving them
Off into darkness. Ask my name.

RIDDLE 15

My throat is white, my head and sides
Tawny yellow. I am armed, and move
Swiftly. My face and back are shaggy
With hair; two ears tower high
Above my eyes; I step through the green   5

Grass on my toes. Misery is certain
Whenever some battle-fierce warrior sniffs me
Out, there where I lie hidden
With my children: we stay in our house when strangers
Come knocking at our doors—death would enter,   10
If I let it. Sometimes, to save young lives
I quietly carry my children off,
Flee from our home: whoever follows me,
Chases along the roads we take,
Goes crawling on his belly. How stupid I would be   15
If I waited for him, and his fury, to find me
At home: no, my running hands
Quickly dig us a path through the hill.
I can save freeborn lives, leading
My family up through a secret tunnel,   20
Up through the tall hill. Safety
Is easy, then; murderous dogs
No longer trouble me. And yet, if a vicious
Enemy tracks me down, wriggling through
Narrow pathways, he'll find the fight   25
He comes hunting, once I've climbed to the top
Of the hill; he'll find me waiting, ready
To hurl darts and javelins at a hated
Opponent, no longer running, or afraid.

RIDDLE 25

I'm a wonderful fellow that women love,
Since their neighbors can use me. No one gets hurt
When they call on me, except the killer
Himself. I rise high over the bed
(But I'm hairy underneath). Sometimes some fellow's   5
Proud and pretty daughter grabs me,
Grips me tight and pulls me up,
Yanks my red head, holds me hard,
Well aware what she's got, knowing what I'm good for
And what's in her hand, as soon as she's near me   10
With her lovely curled hair. And then she cries.

RIDDLE 26

An enemy robbed me of life, stole
My strength, then soaked me in water, dipping me
In and out. He set me in the sun,
And all the hair I had had was gone,
Dried to nothing. A knife's hard edge   5
Ground away my last impurity,
And fingers folded me, and a bird's delight
Spread black drops all over me, walking
Up and down, stopping to swallow
Tree-dye wet with water, then walking   10
Again. Later, a man covered me
With sheltering boards, stretched skin around me,
And dressed me in gold; a smith's glowing
Work was wound across me. Now let
These decorations, this crimson dye,   15
And all this glorious labor celebrate
The Lord, far and near! (—Not punish
The dull, like a penance!) If men will use me
Their souls will be safer, surer of Heaven,
Their hearts bolder, more joyful, their minds   20
Wiser and more knowing. Their friends, their families,
Will be truer, better, more just, more worthy,
More perfect in their faith. Prosperity and honor
And grace will come to them; kindness and mercy
Will circle them round, and love will hold them   25
Tightly in its arms. What am I, so useful
To men? My name is a great one, holy
In itself, famous for the help it can bring.

RIDDLE 28

A low-lying, lovely field carefully
Sown with a stubborn, hard-edged crop
That needs to be cut by the sharpest blades,
Flaked and scraped, tied and dried,
Leached and bleached, pounded and bent,   5

Softened and shined, then carried far off
To the doors of men. There's pleasure hiding
Inside this creature, residing down deep,
Clinging and lingering, lasting long hours,
Nights of delight that no one minds.   10
But later they wonder if the price was right
And death was too much. Even wise men
Must work pretty hard to proclaim its name.

RIDDLE 29

I saw a silvery creature scurrying
Home, as lovely and light as heaven
Itself, running with stolen treasure
Between its horns. It hoped, by deceit
And daring and art, to set an arbor   5
There in that soaring castle. Then,
A shining creature, known to everyone
On earth, climbed the mountains and cliffs,
Rescued his prize, and drove the wily
Impostor back to darkness. It fled   10
To the west, swearing revenge. The morning
Dust scattered away, dew
Fell, and the night was gone. And no one
Knew where the soft-footed thief had vanished.

RIDDLE 32

Our world is lovely in different ways,
Hung with beauty and works of hands.
I saw an ingenious thing, made
For motion, slide against the sand,
Shrieking as it went. It walked swiftly   5
On its only foot, this odd-shaped monster,
Traveled in an open country without
Seeing, without arms, or hands,
With many ribs, and its mouth in its middle.
Its work is useful, and welcome, for it loads   10

Its belly with food, and brings abundance
To men, to poor and to rich, paying
Its tribute year after year. Solve
This riddle, if you can, and unravel its name.

RIDDLE 33

A creature came through the waves, beautiful
And strange, calling to shore, its voice
Loud and deep; its laughter froze
Men's blood; its sides were like sword blades. It swam
Contemptuously along, slow and sluggish,   5
A bitter warrior and a thief, ripping
Ships apart, and plundering. Like a witch
It wove spells—and knew its own nature, shouting:
"My mother is the fairest virgin of a race
Of noble virgins: she is my daughter   10
Grown great. All men know her, and me,
And know, everywhere on earth, with what joy
We will come to join them, to live on land!"

RIDDLE 44

It hangs, elegant, high on his thigh,
Under his shirt, with a hole in the front.
It stands so upright, stiff and hard!
When he takes it out of his clothes, intending
To use it, he'll stick the head of his hanging   5
Thing straight in that matching hole
That he's filled in this way so often before.

RIDDLE 45

I've heard of a something that grows by itself,
Thicker and fatter till it lifts up its covers,
And the girl grabs that boneless what-is-it
In her high-minded hands and shoves that swelling
Thing up under her innocent dress.   5

RIDDLE 47

A worm ate words. I thought that wonderfully
Strange—a miracle—when they told me a crawling
Insect had swallowed noble songs,
A nighttime thief had stolen writing
So famous, so weighty. But the prowler was foolish   5
Still, though its belly was full of thought.

RIDDLE 57

These little creatures come floating along
The mountain breeze. Black as they can be,
Dark all over, singing as they come,
They fly in flocks, tramping through the woods
With their wild cries, and sometimes even   5
Entering men's houses. But they name themselves.

RIDDLE 60

I grew where life had come to me, along
The sandy shore, where the sea foamed in
Below a cliff. Men came
To my empty land only by accident.
But every dawn a brown wave swept   5
Around me with watery arms. How
Could I ever imagine a time when, mouthless,
I'd sing across the benches where mead•
Was poured, and carry secret speech?
What a strange and wonderful thing to someone   10
Who puzzles, but neither sees nor knows,
That the point of a knife and a strong right hand
Should press and carve me, a keen blade
And the mind of a man joined together
To make me a message-bearer to your ears   15
Alone, boldly bringing you what no one
Else could carry and no one hears!

RIDDLE 66

I am greater than all this world, smaller
Than the smallest worm; I walk more softly
Than the moon, swifter than the sun. I hold
Oceans and seas in my arms; the earth's
Green fields lie on my breast. I touch   5
Endless depths, deeper than Hell,
And reach higher than Heaven, further than
The stars and the angels' home. I fill
The earth, the world, and its rushing waters
With myself. Say my name, if you know it.   10

RIDDLE 87

The final lines are missing

What a wonderful creature! Its belly was big
—Lord, it was swollen! A man walked behind it,
A strapping big fellow: he looked to me
Like a powerful fighter. He laid hold of that thing
With Heaven's sharp tooth, the bite of the wind,   5
And blew in its face. And how it barked!
But then it gave up. What he'd really intended . . .

MAXIMS I

I.

　　　Ask me your wisest words!/
　　　　　　　　Don't make your mind a mystery,
Disguising what you know most deeply!/
　　　　　　　　How can I tell you my secrets
If you hide your insights away,/
　　　　　　　keep your heart's thoughts to yourself?
Men who can use their minds/
　　　　　　　must speak them. And first they must praise
God, our wonderful Father,/
　　　　　　　for bringing us to life   5

And giving us freedom of will./
                 He wants us to remember these gifts.
God must live in glory;/
             man must live on earth,
Be young, grow old. But God is always
With us; nothing that happens can change
Or affect Him, the Almighty, neither sickness nor age.   10
His spirit never grows older;/
             He is always as He was,
Our patient Prince. He grants us our minds,
And different temperaments, and ways of speech.
Earth's islands support all manner
Of living creatures—countless lands   15
That Almighty God, our Maker, created
Just for mankind, divided among
All sorts of customs and men. The wise
Must join with the wise, for their minds are alike,
They will settle disputes, and teach men peace,   20
Ending evil wherever it awakens.
Wise men must consult, godly and sagacious,
The good with the good—and women with men,
For husbands and wives bring forth new life
And people the earth. So trees must scatter   25
Leaves on the ground, though the branches mourn them.
Everything ends, we die because
We must, so every day be ready
To leave this world. Only God knows
Exactly where death comes from,/
             and where it takes us when it goes. 30
Life replaces life, when it's lost;
The numbers of men are always the same;
There are never more children than once there were,
But only because He keeps us in check.
    All except fools know God,/
             for who can predict his death? 35
Wise men protect their souls,/
             keep their minds righteous and pure.

The blessèd prosper at home,/
>   the unlucky are betrayed by their friends.
No man can live without food:/
>   need is a fearsome constraint.
An innocent heart is happy./
>   The blind man must long for his eyes,
The loss of what once was clear:/
>   he cannot see the stars,   40
The brightness of sun and moon,/
>   and it hurts him, deep in his heart,
Knowing what he alone knows,/
>   never expecting relief.
But God made him for this pain,/
>   and God can return him his sight,
Heal the jewels in his head,/
>   if He knows the heart is pure.
Men must trust their physician./
>   A young man must be properly taught, 45
Strengthened and stretched into wisdom,/
>   tamed until he learns sense,
Freely fed and clothed/
>   until he's been led into wisdom.
Children must not be discouraged,/
>   but must be given their chance,
For then they will thrive among men,/
>   knowing what they need to know.
Men with bold hearts must be steered./
>   Winds will stir up the ocean, 50
Send its sandy waves/
>   sweeping angry against
The shore, swimming from far out,/
>   testing the land's strength.
But hills and cliffs stand firm,/
>   and slowly calm the wind.
So the sea is still
When the wind blows soft,*
>   55

---

*Lines 54 and 55 are half-lines●, not alliteratively connected; most editors print them, accordingly, as separate lines.

As men will live in peace/
                    when they've patiently settled disputes,
Letting each other prosper,/
                    keeping themselves in order
When bold men know how to rule./
                    Kings always want power,
Dislike whoever wants land,/
                    love whoever gives it.
The glorious are proud, the brave are strong,   60
And both must always be ready for battle.
Knights belong on their warhorse,/
                    cavalry ride in formation,
And soldiers stand on their feet./
                    Women belong at their looms:
A wandering wife makes for scandal,/
                    accused of all kinds of foulness,
Scolded with unpleasant words,/
                    and soon she loses her beauty.   65
The wicked must live in darkness;/
                    honesty loves the light.
The head must control the hands;/
                    treasure must wait to be found;
A throne must be ready for use,/
                    whenever men will award it.
Men who get gold are greedy,/
                    but a king on his throne has enough:
We need to pay back what we're given,/
                    unless we prefer to be liars.   70

II.

      Frost must freeze, fire eat wood,
Ground grow green, ice make icicles,
Water make waves, earth's seeds
Seal like miracles. Only Almighty
God can dissolve the frost's hard chains,   75
Drive away winter, bring back good weather,
Summer's hot skies, the changeable seas.
Death's deep road is the darkest of secrets,
But the corpse must be burned, and the dead man's goods

Divided. The best thing of all is glory.   80
Kings must buy their brides with cups
And cattle and rings, and queens, too,
Must be open-handed. The man must be used
To war; the woman must learn to be loved
By her people, always pleasant, known   85
To keep her own secrets and give away horses
And jewels with a smile, a helpful presence
At mead-hall• councils, well aware
Of which men must be greeted first,
And how her husband, ruler of the land,   90
Deserves deference, and help him with advice
To preserve their reign, the two together.
          Ships need nails, and shields need ropes,
To be held together, and a Frisian husband's
Wife should welcome him home from a voyage,   95
As his ship lands and her man returns,
Bringing her bread, and she leads him in,
Washes his sea-stained clothes,/
                              and offers him fresh, clean new ones,
                         And takes him to bed, as his love desires.
Women must honor their vows,/
                    though men will accuse them of foulness,   100
And many women are faithful,/
                         though many like to be false
With strangers, when their men are away,/
                         too far from home to be watching.
Sailors can be long at sea;/
                    they, too, must remember their love,
Wait for what cannot be hurried./
                         And when he's allowed to return
He'll be home, if he knows he's awaited,/   105
                         except when waves hold him back,
For a seagoing husband is the water's hostage.
But a ship coming home from successful sailing
Can buy a man kingdoms, whatever he wants,
Lakes and lands to enjoy,/
                    dwellings where the traveler can rest,

And all the food he can eat,/   110
                     for as long as his appetite lasts—
For a man must eat to be healthy,/
                     and even set in the sun
A sick man's oppressed by the weather,/
                     summer's warmth is worthless,
He'll fade, and soon he'll die,/
                     unless he puts food in his stomach.
Strength is fed by food,/
                     but sin lies in the ground,
Hidden in the earth, covered away.   115
Death is indecent, when it's kept in the dark.
      The humble will bow, the low sink lower,
And justice will flourish, for wisdom is profit,
And none of their sins will help the ignorant.
For God rules, and will always rule.   120
Contain your mind, control your hand;
The eye sees, but understanding
Is in the heart, where thought arises.
Everyone's mouth must be fed,/
                     and meals should be on time.
Gold bèlongs on a soldier's sword   125
And his victory robes, like jewels on a queen;
Warriors find poets and war important,
For peace depends on successful battles.
Soldiers need shields, and robbers spears;
Brides need rings, and books must be read;   130
Christ's blood's for the holy, and sin is for heathens•.
Old Woden• made idols, but God Almighty
Made the world and the skies, the King of Heaven,
The Lord of Truth, Savior of souls,
Who gave us all we have and live on,   135
And once again, at the end of time,
Will hold us in His hand. For He is the Lord.

III.
      Speak wisely, when you speak; write in runes•, if you write.
Poems should be sung, praise should be earned;

Live life fully, and remember glory.   140
A sensible man can spot a sensible
Horse, with good round hooves, and its head
In the front; no man can earn too much.
A man should be sure of friends,/
                    no matter which road he follows,
Not needing to avoid a town/   145
               where he knows there's no one to trust.
A miserable, friendless man/
                will find himself traveling with wolves,
Deceitful beasts who turn and bite:
Be as wary of the gray one as dead men of the grave;
It will howl with hunger, but not in mourning,
And never worries when men are destroyed: 150
No matter how many die, it wants more.
      A wound needs a bandage, and a hard man revenge;
A bow needs an arrow; both arrow and bow
Must be matched with a man. Treasure depends
On treasure; gold must be given. God   155
Gives to the rich, then takes His gifts back.
Mead-halls endure, though buildings are old.
Fallen trees are unlikely to grow,
And in order to grow a tree must sprout branches,
As honest faith must sprout in the heart.   160
But foolish, faithless, reckless men,
False and filled with venom,
Are not guided by God.*
In the beginning, the Almighty/
              made us all, and we move as He made us.
No man is immune from the need to speak wisely,   165
Poets in their songs, warriors in their wisdom.
The earth offers us different/
               minds, and different men,

*Lines 161–163 are metrically irregular. I have tried to indicate this in the translation by giving line 162 three instead of four stresses, and giving line 161 only two stresses—a sort of descending progression which, as (in the original Old English) it is perhaps intended to do, helps emphasize the extended (hypermetric•) line that immediately follows.

And each understands in his own way.
Men who remember many poems,
Or can make harp• strings sing, are happier,   170
For the gift of music is sent from God.
But the man who lives alone is miserable:
Fate has ordained that his life must be friendless.
Life would be better if he had/

                   a brother, and they shared one father,
Sons of some noble man:/

               if they had to hunt the wild boar   175
They'd protect one another from the fearsome beast,
And always advise and take counsel together,
And sleep in one bed,
Forever at peace
Until they die.*   180
They can sit at chess together,/

               and slowly forget their anger,
Forgive harsh words and deeds/

                 in the calm good-cheer of the game,
For there's time to relax and forget/

                  in such casual pleasures at home,
But not in a ship at sea,/

               except when it runs at full sail:
Rowing against the wind/   185

               is wearying, and tempers can flare,
And a man accused of laxness/

               may lift his oar from the sea.
Deceit goes with corruption and cunning;
Jewels can be stolen.
Men will bicker
When their backs are turned,   190
But the wise man is ready.†

*Lines 178–180 are half-lines, and—once again—are followed by hypermetric lines. For a discussion of this imperfectly understood practice, see Burton Raffel, "*Judith:* Hypermetricity and Rhetoric," in *Anglo-Saxon Poetry,* ed. Lewis E. Nicholson and Dolores Warwick Freese (Notre Dame, Ind.: Notre Dame University Press, 1975), 124–134.

†Lines 188–191 are metrically aberrant, as well as deeply obscure. Once again, unusually shortened lines are followed by unusually lengthened ones.

Men have been feuding forever,/
                               since the earth first swallowed the blood
Of Abel, killed by Cain./
                        That was no one-day evil,
For those angry drops spattered all over,
In ancient times, spreading malice   195
Far and wide. Cain killed his own brother,
But couldn't keep murder for himself:/
                               other men followed his lead,
And practiced his craft, and mankind suffered.
Weapons were used all over the world,
Swords were invented, fashioned for destruction.   200
Shields must be ready, spears kept straight,
Sword blades sharp, and spear points piercing.
Men's minds must be ready, and the brave man's helmet,
But a coward's heart has no room for courage.

THE FORTUNES OF MEN

    How often it happens, given God's powers,
That husband and wife beget a child,
And bring him into the world, and clothe him
Brightly, and encourage and teach him, till the time
Comes, as the years pass, that he's grown,   5
Quickened with life, become a man.
Father and mother lead and guide him,
Feed and prepare him. But God alone knows
What the turning cycle of seasons will bring!
    Some have barely matured, are still young,   10
When, alas! their worldly worries are over,
Their lives ended. Wandering wolves
Feed on their flesh, and their mothers mourn
Their death. No man can control such things!
    Some will die of famine;/
                            storms sweep others away;   15
Some will be pierced by spears;/
                         some are destroyed by war.

Some will live with no sight in their eyes,
Groping with their hands; some will be lame,
Muscles crippled, moaning in pain,
Mourning their fate, their hearts afflicted.   20
Some will fall, wingless, from high
Trees in the forest, waving their arms
And trying to fly, till no more branches
Can keep them in the air. Then they reach the roots
And are left unconscious; the soul leaves   25
As they come to the ground, and flies on its way.
　　　Some must walk, alone, in faraway
Places, carrying their food on their back,
Trudging through mud in barbarian lands,
Among alien people, mostly unwelcome,   30
With few to help, mistrusted everywhere
For their hard and weary, homeless lives.
　　　Others will swing from the high gallows,
Hang till they're dead, and soul, and life
Have left the bloody, broken body.   35
And ravens will pluck the eyes from their heads,
Black-feathered birds tear at corpses
That no longer have hands to defend themselves
From flying robbers, for life has fled
And bodies feel nothing, hopeless and cold,   40
Hanging bloodless, pallid, wrapped
In death's mist. Their very names become curses!
　　　Some are condemned to die in the fire,
Doomed men eaten by fierce flames,
Death coming quickly as the wild red roaring   45
Leaps and flares, and women weep,
Watching their children devoured by embers.
　　　Some, swilling ale, and angry,
Soaked in wine, will meet death
At the edge of a sword, for their hasty words.   50
　　　And some, when stewards fill their cups
Too freely, will like it too much, and lose
All balance, and their mouths will rule their brains,

And they'll drink their miserable lives away
In suffering and pain, all pleasure gone;   55
Men will say they killed themselves,
And tell tall tales of their wild drinking.
     And some, with God's good help, will finish
Wasting their days before they're mature
And, older, will be happy again, and rich,   60
And live their lives in peace and prosperity,
In the midst of their families, joyful and content
For as long as any man's pleasures may last.
     And thus Almighty God parcels
Out men's lives across the earth,   65
Ordaining, prescribing, shaping our fates,
Wealth for some, for others misery,
Making young men happy, glorious
In war, distributing splendid skills,
Awarding honors at swift-handed dice   70
And crafty chess games. Some grow learned,
Ripe in wisdom. Some are given
Wonderful gifts, working in gold,
Always hammering heated metal
For some kingly mail shirt, repaid by their lords   75
With open hands, happy and welcome.
     Some will appear where men come crowding,
Drinking and merry as they sit at their benches,
A host of happy tipplers. Harps•
Will be played by some, sitting at their lords'   80
Feet, well-paid for their songs, plucking
Swift and skillful at the tight-strung strings,
Their fingers dancing, now soft, now loud,
Making magnificent music come forth.
     Some will tame proud wild birds,   85
Bring hawks to their hands, turn fierce falcons
Proud of their wings, into toys of pleasure,
With rings on their legs, fed in their fetters,
Swift birds coaxed with bits of food
Until the killer belongs to his keeper,   90

Will do as he's told, trained to obedience,
A servant sitting in his master's hand.
    And so the Savior of men works
His will across the earth, carefully
Shapes and guides our hearts and minds,   95
Assigns to each of us a path and a fate.
Let all men thank Him and praise His name,
For the infinite mercies He gives to mankind.

PHYSIOLOGUS

*A "Bestiary": two of three poems. The third, "The Partridge," is badly
mangled; in fact, so much is missing that the subject "partridge" is only a
dubious conjecture.*

1. THE PANTHER

    There are too many beasts roaming this middle
Earth for us ever to tell
Their noble traits, or even to count them.
Birds and animals are scattered all over
The world, moving far and wide   5
In every direction, like the water circling
The earth's surface, the roaring oceans,
The salt waves beating. Of one such wild
And wonderful creature we've heard it said
That he roams a famous and faraway land,   10
Guarding his home, choosing to dwell
In mountain caves. The animal's name
Is "panther," according to the sons of men,
The wise scholars, who've written about
That wandering beast. He's said to be friendly,   15
Kind to men, but dangerous to dragons,
Showing eternal hatred to serpents
For all the evil those creatures can do.
    He's a beautiful beast, with a coat shining
With every color—as pious men   20
Have said that Joseph's coat was dyed

With each of the colors men can weave
Into cloth, and all glittering and gleaming
In the eyes of men brighter than any
Ever seen, so too this panther   25
Glows with all the colors in the world,
Each more vivid, shining more
Intense and magnificent, each still lovelier
Than the other, dazzling treasures forever
Stranger and more marvelous. He lives by himself,   30
Gentle, modest, kind, humane,
Loving and lovable, unwilling to injure
Anything but that poisonous reptile,
His ancient enemy, as I mentioned before.
Forever thankful for a full stomach,   35
After eating he seeks peaceful sleep
In some secret place, deep in the mountains,
Where this mighty warrior rests and dreams
For three whole days, totally dormant,
Then suddenly wakes up again   40
From his three-day sleep, bold and ready,
Stronger than ever. He throws back his head
And roars out wondrous sounds. And once
He's given voice, his mouth emits
A rare fragrance, a joyous breath,   45
The sweetest and strongest scent, lovelier
Than garden herbs and forest flowers,
Finer and nobler than all earth's treasures.
And then bands of warriors flock from throne rooms
And castles, cities and towns, hordes   50
Of armored, spear-bearing men following
Far-flung roads, and birds and beasts
Among them, having heard the voice and hurrying,
Now, to find and savor that scent.
        Just so is righteous God, dispenser   55
Of joy, generous with all other creatures,
Eternally open-handed, except
With serpents, those sources of poison—the ancient

Enemy, sealed into depths of torment,
Locked and chained in the fires of Hell,   60
Smothered in pain—just so He rose
From darkness, on the third day, Giver
Of Glory, Prince of Angels, having suffered
Death for us, and spread His sweet
And glorious fragrance all through the world.   65
And forever after, crowds of the faithful
Have hurried toward Him, from every side,
Seeking that fragrance all over the world.
For as Saint Paul, the wise, has told us:
"How various and many are the ways that God,   70
Father Almighty, and our only hope,
Has chosen to give us, here on this earth,
As high in Heaven, to preserve the lives
Of all His creatures." What a noble fragrance!

2. THE WHALE

        And now let me sing you, with whatever wordcraft
Skill my limited mind can master,
The song of a fish, the mighty whale.
Sailors often meet him by accident,
On distant seas, fierce and savage,   5
Forever dangerous. This floater on oceans
Is known by the name "Fastitocalon."*
He looks like a huge and scabby stone,
The sort that crumbles at the edge of the sea,
A vast bank surrounded by sand,   10
So travelers crossing the swelling waves
Imagine that what they see is an island,
And sometimes tie their high-prowed ships
To this land-not-land, which can change in a moment,
Moor their seahorses where the waters seem   15
To end, and then march boldly out
Of their ships, down on the island, leaving

*Bad Greek for "tortoise-shield."

The bound-up boats rocking in the tide.
Tired of traveling, weary at heart,
Suspecting nothing, they make their camp,   20
Kindle a flame, and light themselves
A blazing bonfire, happy and relaxed,
Weary and wanting only their rest.
And when he feels them secure and off guard,
This cunning, wicked creature, warrior   25
Of the sea, suddenly plunges below
The waves, deep in the salty water,
Boldly dragging with him, straight
To the bottom, ships and men and all,
Down to a deathly cavern where everything   30
Drowns in his grip. These are devils' tricks,
The work of fiends, using the strength
They so carefully hide to deceive mankind,
Transforming all good deeds into evil,
Turning men's minds and hearts toward anger,   35
Learning from their enemy, till they're tightly tied
To the house of bad faith where they've chosen to dwell.
And when the faithless fiend, buried
In living torment, knows for sure
He has a man caught in his snare,   40
Trapped in his noose, he turns his evil
Craft to life-destruction, for proud
And lowborn alike, making them work
His evil lust, then swiftly, using
His invisible power, drawing those beings   45
Emptied of goodness to endlessly boiling,
Mist-dark Hell, exactly as the great
Whale drags down sailors and the wave-steeds
They ride on the sea. And he can do more,
This proud rusher through water, even more   50
Marvelous. When hunger afflicts him, there
In the waves, and the monster longs for food,
This lord of the oceans opens his mouth,
Stretches his lips, and a wondrous scent
Pours from inside him, and that fragrance bewitches   55

Other fish swimming in the sea,
And they come as fast as they can to where
They can find it. They come crowding around him,
Suspecting nothing, until those gaping
Jaws are stuffed and come smashing down,   60
Bitter teeth suddenly closing
On his helpless guests. And so it is
With men, who so often fail to take care of
The lives we've been lent for so short a time,
And let themselves be tricked by sweet scents,   65
Empty desires, and sins stain
Their immortal souls. The devil opens
The doors of Hell when they leave this earth,
For they've foolishly valued fleshly pleasure
More than the heart's duties, and done   70
Evil. And when the wicked fiend,
Sly and deceitful, has them in his fortress,
Those who loved him, burning in his flames,
Chained by their sins, who during their lifetimes
Eagerly did his bidding, and now   75
Have suffered death's final pangs, he savagely
Shuts the gates of Hell behind them,
Closes those jaws from which no one escapes,
Nor ever exits, once they have entered,
No more than swimming fish can ever   80
Return, once the whale has caught them.
And so it is . . . .*

The Lord of all lords denies the Devil,
In word and deed, to bring us to the sight
Of the King of Glory. Let us turn our faces   85
To Him, in our time on earth, and seek
Salvation, eternal love in Heaven,
Safe in the love of Him we love.

---

*There is a sharp break in the sense here, though no apparent break in the physical manuscript.

CHARM FOR BEWITCHED LAND

MS Cotton Caligula A.viii, lines 69–71

Soil, be well again.
Earth, mother of men,
Let God fulfill you with food, be ripe
And fruitful, and give us life.

Prose

PATERNOSTER

Fæder ure, þu þe eart on heofonum, si þin nama
gehalgod. Tobecume þin rice. Gewurþe ðin willa
on eorðan swa swa on heaofonum. Urne gedæghwamlican
hlaf syle us to dæg. And forgyf us ure gyltas, swa swa we
forgyfað urum gyltendum. And ne gelæd þu us on costnunge,
ac alys us of yfele. Soþlice.

Old English Prose

A substantial amount of Old English prose has survived. That with
the most literary merit is religious in nature. Much of the prose—
including wills, charters, and legal texts—is documentary rather
than literary, of principal interest to historians. A greater amount
of this kind of prose survives in Old English than in any other
European vernacular. Also extant is some late Old English prose
dealing with scientific matters, such as Aelfric's translation of Bede's
study of the tides, and herbal and medical books that display a
considerable knowledge of plants. Included here are samples of the
nonliterary genres that provide a necessary background for the litera-
ture, including history, religious texts, laws, wills, and charms. Be-
cause we have not attempted a comprehensive survey, this collection
somewhat resembles King Alfred's translation of Saint Augustine's
Soliloquies: it is *Blostma,* "Blossom-Gatherings."

Historical Prose

THE ANGLO-SAXON CHRONICLE

Chronicles among the Anglo-Saxons probably had their origin with
the Easter Tables, long lists kept by the clergy and used for computing
the date of Easter. It became customary to note the major events of
each year in the margins, and these notations developed into true
annals. In the year 891, a compiler—presumably a cleric in King
Alfred's service—used various sources (earlier annalistic material,
genealogies, Bede's *History,* and oral reports) to write a set of annals
devoted to the history of the English from their settlement of Brit-
ain to the year of compilation. The copies were circulated to various
monasteries, where they continued to be updated. Seven manuscripts
of the chronicle have survived.

Many of the entries contain factual information only (such as
the death of a king), but some contain material of greater liter-
ary interest. The brief entry for the year 793 tells of the portents
(including dragons) over Northumbria that accompanied the Vikings'
destruction of Lindisfarne.

The entry for the year 449 is stirring and is an important source
for our knowledge of the Anglo-Saxon conquest. It describes the
invitation King Vortigern of Britain gave the Germanic tribes and

the coming of the Angles, Saxons, and Jutes. One of the most famous
entries, placed under the year 755 but recording events that occurred
thirty-one years later, is often called "Cynewulf and Cyneheard" after
the names of the protagonists. The entry records a dynastic struggle
between two branches of the West Saxon royal house. The central
themes of this presumably historical work—exile, loyalty, and the
duty of vengeance—are also those found in Old English poetry.

A.D. 449

In this year Martianus and Valentinius became the emperors of Rome,
and ruled for seven winters•. And it was in their time that Hengest
and Horsa, invited by Vortigern, king of the Britons•, arrived in Brit-
ain at the place known as Ebbsfleet, at first to assist the Britons, but
afterward fighting against them. King Vortigern gave them land in
the southeast of this country, on condition that they were to fight
against the Picts•. They did, and were victorious everywhere they
went. Then they sent messages to the Angles, telling them to send
more warriors and telling them the Britons were good-for-nothings
but the land was first-rate. So more warriors were sent. They came
from three Germanic tribes, the Old Saxons, the Angles, and the
Jutes. From the Jutes came the people of Kent and the Isle of Wight—
that is, the people who now live on on the Isle of Wight, and those
West Saxons who, to this day, are known as Jutish folk. From the Old
Saxons came the East Saxons, the South Saxons, and the West Saxons.
From Anglen[, in Denmark,] which afterwards lay desolate between
the Jutes and the Saxons, came the East Angles, Middle Angles, the
Mercians, and all the Northumbrians. Their leaders were a pair of
brothers, Hengest and Horsa, who were the sons of Wihtgils. Wiht-
gils was the son of Witta, who was the son of Wecta, who was the
son of Woden, so that our entire royal line, and also that of the people
living south of the River Humber, is descended from this Woden.

A.D. 754

In this year Cuthred* [King of the West Saxons] died; and Cyneheard
received the bishopric of Winchester, following after Hunferth; and
in this year Canterbury was destroyed by fire; and Sigeberht took
possession of the West Saxon kingdom and remained ruler for a single
year.

A.D. 755

In this year Cynewulf and the West Saxon Witan• took Sigeberht's
kingdom away from him, except for Hampshire, on account of
the evil and unlawful things he had done, and he held Hampshire
until he murdered the ealdorman• who had most determinedly
supported him[, Cumbra], after which Cynewulf drove him into the
Wood of Andred, where he lived until, in revenge for the killing of
Cumbra, a swineherd stabbed him to death, near the River Privett.
And Cynewulf fought many huge battles with the Britons•. And
when he had held the kingdom for about thirty-one years, he meant
to drive from his realm an atheling• whose name was Cyneheard,
who was Sigeberht's brother. But when Cyneheard discovered that
the king, with a few of his followers, had gone to Meretun to be with
his mistress, he rode there after him and, before the men who were
with the king became aware of his presence, surrounded the place.
And when the king realized this, he went to the door and, without
any hesitation, began to defend himself, until, seeing Cyneheard, he
rushed directly out and badly wounded him, and then all of them
fought with the king until they killed him. And then the woman's
screaming alerted the king's men to the disturbance, and they hurried
to the king as quickly as they could make themselves ready, and the
atheling• offered to reward each and all of them with money and
their lives, but none of them would listen to him, but fought until
they all lay dead except for a single British• hostage•, and he was

*Note, as an illustration of the requirement that sons' names alliterate with
their fathers', that the first King of the West Saxons of whom we have any record,
in the sixth century, was Cerdric (whose name is invoked in the last sentence,
below); Cerdric's grandson was name Cynric, and Cynric's son was named
Ceawlin.

badly wounded. Then, in the morning, the king's followers who
had been left behind heard that the king had been slain, and his
ealdormen, Osric and Wigferth, together with all who had been left
behind, rode there, and learned that the atheling who had killed the
king had not left the place, and had locked the gates against them.
So they went there, and the atheling offered them wealth and lands,
and whatever terms they wanted, if they'd let him have the kingdom,
and told them that kinsmen of theirs were with him and would not
desert him, and they told him that none of their kinsmen were dearer
to them than their lord,* and they would never serve and follow the
man who had killed him. And they informed their kinsmen that they
could leave, unharmed, and their kinsmen replied that exactly the
same terms had been offered, earlier, to their comrades who'd been
with the king, and said that they would not pay any more attention
to the offer than had those who'd died alongside the king. And then
they fought on both sides of the gates until they got in and killed
the atheling and all the men who were with him, all except one,
who was ealdorman Osric's godson, whose life was saved, though
he'd been much wounded. Cynewulf had ruled for thirty-one years,
and his body lies in Winchester, and the atheling's in Axminster, and
they are directly descended, in the paternal line, all the way back to
Cerdric. . . .

A.D. 793

In this year terrible signs were seen in the skies over Northumberland,
and people were horribly afraid. There was incredible lightning, and
fierce winds, and fierce dragons could be seen flying through the air.
And right after this there was a great famine, and not long thereafter,
in the same year, on the eighth day of June, alas! plundering heathens•
destroyed God's church at Lindisfarne, robbing and murdering.

---

*Charles Plummer's 1899 edition of the *Chronicle* notes, at this point, that "the
tie of the comitatus supersedes that of the kin; the comitatus forms as it were an
artificial family with its leader as 'father and lord.' So [too] the monastery is an
artificial family."

Testamentary and Legal Prose

OLD ENGLISH WILLS

Charters are documents recording or directing transfers of land
and other property. Those dealing with the transfer of land are be-
tween a king and the Church, or a king and a nobleman, or private
transactions between nonclerics; in addition to transferring land,
wills may also bequeath personal property. These documents are
of historical interest in part because of their lists of witnesses;
Ealdorman• Elfheah's will, for example, is witnessed by "Edthelfryth,
the king's wife," among others, showing that women witnessed legal
transactions. The will of King Alfred is historically significant (it
identifies the crown estates•) and shows us that the king was aware
of his obligations to his kin, his nobles, the Church, and the poor.
The other wills translated here contain lists of possessions bequeathed
and show us something about the lives of the nobility. Wulfwaru's
concern with bequeathing women's clothing and headbands to her
kinswomen gives us a poignant glimpse of Old English life that is
made more moving because neither Wulfwaru nor her children have
been identified.

KING ALFRED'S WILL

I, Alfred, king by the grace of God, after consultation with Arch-
bishop Ethelred, in the presence of all the members of the Witan•
of this West Saxon realm, have been reflecting on the needs of my
soul, and considering the inheritance given me by God and my
forefathers, and also the inheritance that King Ethelwulf, my father,
bequeathed to his sons—Ethelbald, Ethelred, and me—and which
we three brothers had agreed should go in its entirety to the one
who lived the longest. But, as it happened, Ethelbald passed away.
And Ethelred and I, in the presence of the Witan of this West Saxon
realm, entrusted our share to our kinsman, King Ethelbert, on con-
dition that he would afterward return it to us exactly as it had been
when we committed it to his care—as he then did, and not only
the inheritance, but also what he had obtained from the use of what
Ethelred and I shared in common, as well as what he himself had
earned. And then Ethelred became king, and I asked him, in the
presence of all the members of the Witan, to divide our inheritance
and give me my share. Then he told me he could not easily make
such a division, for indeed he had already made the attempt many
times, and he said, as follows: After his death there was no one but me
to whom he would rather bequeath both our common inheritance
and whatever he himself had acquired. And I was well contented
with that.

But as it happened we were all set upon by the heathen•. And he
and I talked about our children, for no matter what befell us, in our
troubles, they would need property of their own. We were holding
a council at Swinbeorg. And we agreed, he and I, in the presence
of all the members of the Witan of this realm, that whichever of
us lived the longest should give the other's children both the lands
we had either of us acquired and also the lands which our father,
King Ethelwulf, had given us individually, while Ethelbald was still
alive, but not including the inheritance he had bequeathed to us
jointly. And we gave each other our promise: whichever of us lived
the longest should have all the land and treasure we both possessed,
except whatever share we each had left to our children.

Then Ethelred died, and no one made known to me any will, or
any oral testament, which in any way contradicted the arrangement

which, in front of witnesses, we two had previously agreed upon. But there were many disputes among the heirs. Accordingly, I brought King Ethelwulf's will to our council meeting at Langdon, and had it read out in the presence of all the members of the Witan of this realm. And when it had been read, I asked them all, for love of me (and gave them my word I would never reproach any of them for speaking the truth), not to shrink from affirming the common law, either from love or from fear of me, lest anyone say I had injured my kinsmen, either the old or the young. And then they unanimously declared and said, and correctly, that they could not think of anyone who had a better claim, nor could they perceive anything of the sort in the will. "Now that it has all come into your possession," they said, "you are entitled to bequeath and bestow it to anyone, kinsman or stranger, however you may choose." And each and all promised me, and affixed their signatures to that pledge, that as long as they lived no one would ever change or overturn whatever disposition of that property I myself might make, when I came to my last day.

THEREFORE: I, Alfred, king of the West Saxons, by the grace of God and in the presence of these witnesses, do hereby declare how I wish to bequeath my inheritance, once I am dead. First, I give to Edward, my oldest son, the land at Stratton in Triggshire, and in Hartland, and the entire entailed• estate• held by Leofheah, and the land at Carhampton and at Kilton and at Burnham and at Wedmore, along with the land at Chewton and what is thereunto belonging. And I most earnestly request the community of religious at Cheddar that they choose him, according to the agreement they and I have previously made. And I give him the land at Cannington and at Bedwyn and at Pewsey and at Hurstbourne and at Sutton and at Leatherhead and at Alton.

And all the entailed land that I have in Kent and at lower Hurstbourne and at Chiseldon, and the private estate in lower Hurstbourne which I entrusted to Ecgwulf, shall be returned to Winchester, according to the terms under which my father had earlier bequeathed it.

And to my younger son [I give] the land at Arreton, and that at Dean, and that at Meon and at Amesbury and at Dean and at Sturminster and at Yeovil and at Crewkerne and at Whitchurch and at Axmouth and at Branscombe and at Cullompton and at Tiverton and at Milborne and at Exminster and at Sothworth and at Lifton,

and all the lands belonging thereto—that is to say, everything I have
in Cornwall, with the exception of Triggshire.

And to my oldest daughter [, Ethelflad, I give] the estate at Wellow.

And to my middle daughter [, Ethelgift, I give] the estate at
Kingsclere and that at Candover.

And to my youngest daughter [, Ethelrift, I give] the estate at
Welig, and that at Ashton, and that at Chippanham.

And to Ethelhelm, my brother's son, [I give] the estate at Alding-
bourne, and that at Compton, and that at Crondall, and that at
Beeding, and that at Beddingham, and that at Burnham, and that at
Thunderfield, and that at Eashing.

And to my brother's son, Ethelwold, [I give] the estate at Godal-
ming, and that at Guildford, and that at Steyning.

And to Osferth, my kinsman, [I give] the estate at Beckley, and
that at Rotherfield, and that at Ditchling, and that at Sutton, and that
at Lyminster, and that at Angmering, and that at Felpham, with the
lands belonging thereto.

And [I give] to Ealswith the estate at Lambourn, and that at
Wantage, and that at Edington.

And [I give] to my two sons [jointly the sum of] one thousand
pounds, five hundred pounds to each; and to my oldest daughter,
and to my middle daughter, and to my youngest daughter, and [also]
to Ealswith, [I give jointly the sum of] four hundred pounds, one
hundred pounds to each; and to each of my ealdormen• [I give] one
hundred mancus• coins, and the same to Ethelhelm and Ethelwold
and to Osferth; and [I give] to Ealdorman Ethered a sword worth one
hundred mancus coins. And to the men who serve me,* and to whom,
at Easter, I have recently given money, I leave [the sum of] two
hundred pounds, to be divided among them in such proportions (as
established at Easter) as are owing to each. And [I give] one hundred
mancus coins to the archbishop, and also to Bishop Esne, and to
Bishop Waeferth, and to the bishop of Sherbourne.

And in my name, and in my father's, and the friends for whom
my father used to have prayers said, and for whom I have similarly
interceded, [I give the sum of] two hundred pounds, fifty of which

---

*The king had three companies of personal attendants, each company serving
one month at a time.

is for the priests throughout my kingdom, fifty of which is for poor servants of God, fifty pounds of which is for the needy poor, and fifty of which is for the church in which I am laid to rest.

And I am not sure whether there is this much money, or whether there is more (though I think there is). And if indeed there is more, let it be shared among those to whom I have bequeathed money. And I direct that my ealdormen and those who have served me are all to be included [in this distribution] and are to see to it that such monies are distributed as I have directed.

Since I had previously given different testamentary directions about my property, at a time when I had more property, and more kinsmen, and had entrusted these earlier wills to many men, in the presence of whom they were written, I have now burned all such documents that I was able to lay my hands on. If any such are found, they are to be disregarded, for it is my wish that, now, with God's help, my property shall be dealt with as herein stated.

And I direct that those who hold land according to the provisions of my father's will shall adhere thereto, to the extent possible. And if I have unpaid debts to anyone, I most emphatically wish my kinsmen to pay them.

And I direct those to whom I have bequeathed my entailed estates not to let them pass out of my family, upon their deaths, but, rather, unless any of them have children, that such lands go to my nearest kin, in which case I prefer the heir to be on the paternal side, provided that there be a fitting heir. My grandfather bequeathed his lands to the paternal rather than to the maternal line, so if I have left anything my grandfather owned to someone on the female side, I direct that my kinsmen, if they wish to have such property during their lifetimes, either buy it back or wait until the death of such persons, at which time it shall pass as herein provided. I stipulate that they pay for any such property so that I myself may give either to the female or to the male side, as I choose.

And I pray, in the name of God and His saints, that no kinsman or heir of mine trouble any dependent* for whom I have paid and the

---

* *Cyrelif,* literally, "someone with a choice of life." According to Bosworth and Toller's *Anglo-Saxon Dictionary,* "On decease of a lord, the cultivators [farmers] choose a lord for themselves." As Dorothy Whitelock says, "Not all powerful men

legal disposition of whom was given to me by the West Saxon Witan, so that I could either let them be free or not free, as I chose, but for love of God and for my own soul I cannot help but declare them free and able to choose for themselves, and I beg in the name of the living God that no man oppress them, neither with claims for the payment of money nor in any other way, in order to keep them from choosing to serve whomever they please.

And I desire, both for my own sake and for the sake of Elflade, and for the sake of those for whom she used to pray and I, too, prayed, that the religious community at Damerham be given title to their lands and the freedom to choose the lord they prefer. And from among my herds let such payment be made, for the sake of my soul, as it may be possible to make, and as it may seem fitting and proper to make, and as you may be prepared to render on my behalf.

ELFGIFU'S WILL

c. 966–975

This is what Elfgifu asks of her sovereign lord. She beseeches him, for love of God and for his own royal honor, that she be allowed to make her will.

And next she makes known to you what, with your approval, she wishes to give to God's church, for you and for your soul. And first, that she gives to the old monastery (where she desires her body may rest) the estate• at Risborough, exactly as it is, except that, with your approval, she wishes that, in each town and village, every subject of hers, enslaved for the commission of a crime, be freed. And she gives two hundred gold mancus• coins to said old monastery, and the coffer• containing her holy relics. And she gives to the new monastery the estate at Bledlow, and a hundred gold mancus coins. And [she gives] to the nunnery a dish upon which the Eucharist• is served, and [she gives] the estate at Whaddon to the church of Christ and [the Benedictine nunnery of] Saint Mary at Romsey, and [she gives the estate] at Chesham to [the monastery at] Abingdon, and [the estate] at Wickham to [the monastery at] Bath.

---

were scrupulous in observing the rights of weaker individuals" (*Beginnings of English Society*, 99).

And I give to my sovereign lord the estates at Wing, Linslade, Haversham, Hatfield, Masworth, and Gussage, and two bracelets, each worth one hundred and twenty mancus coins, and a sop-cup•, and six horses, and an equal number of shields and spears. And [I give] to the prince the estate at Newnham, and a bracelet worth thirty mancus coins. And [I give] the queen a necklace worth one hundred and twenty mancus coins, and a bracelet worth thirty mancus coins, and a sop-cup. And to Bishop Ethelwold I give the estate at Taefersceat. And I ask him not to cease praying for my mother and for me. And with my sovereign lord's approval I give the estates at Mongewell and Berkhampstead, in common, to Elfweard and Ethelweard and Elfwaru, to hold during their lifetimes, said estates after their death to go to the old monastery, on behalf of my sovereign lord and me. And, so long as they hold these estates, they are to pay to the two monasteries, each year, two days' worth of food [for the entire community].

And I release my sister, Elfwaru, from having to repay all I have lent her.* And [I give] Ethelflad, my brother's wife, the headband† I lent her.

And to each abbot [I give] five pounds of pennies,‡ for the repair of their monasteries.

And with your approval, my dear lord, I wish that anything which may be left over be given in trust to the bishop [of Winchester] and to Abbot Ethelgar [of the new monastery], for the repair of their holy houses, and so that they may distribute to the poor, on my behalf, such sums as may seem to them most good and useful.

And I beg my sovereign lord, for the love of God, not to forsake any of my men who seek his protection, and seem to him worthy.

And I give Elfweard a sop-cup and Ethelweard an ornamented drinking-horn.

---

*Literally, "And I give Elfwaru, my sister, everything I have lent her."

†"Baend" can mean "crown, chaplet, head-ornament"; the "headband" in question was probably a good deal more costly than an ordinary "headband" would be today.

‡The "penny" was a silver coin, worth a fifth of a shilling and a thirtieth of a mancus.

EALDORMAN ELFHEAH'S WILL

c. 968–971

Here in this document Ealdorman• Elfheah sets forth how he has declared, with his sovereign lord's approval, his last will and testament.

First, for the sake of his soul he gives to his said lord the estate• at Ellendun, and [he gives] that at Crondall to the old monastery at Winchester. And [he gives] the twenty hides* at Charlton to the town of Malmesbury, and the fifteen hides at Sutton to [the town of] Bath, and [he gives] to his sovereign lord the hundred and twenty hides at Worth, and the estates at Cookham, Thatcham, Chelsworth, and that at Inglesham, and at Aylesbury, and Wendover, and [also] three hundred gold mancus• coins, and a dish worth three pounds,† and a sop-cup• worth three pounds, and a dagger, the hilt of which is worth eighty gold mancus coins, and six swords, and six horses with their harnesses, and the same number of spears and shields.

And he gives to his aunt Elthyth, the king's wife, the estate at Sherbourne, exactly as it is. And [he gives] to the older prince, the king's son and hers, thirty gold mancus coins and a sword. And [he gives] to the younger prince the estate at Walkhampstead.

And to Elfhere, his brother, he gives the estates at Faringdon and Aldbourne.

And to Godwin, his son, [he gives] the estate at Tudingatum.

And to Elfweard [he gives] the estate at Wyrton.

And to his kinsman Ethelweard [he gives] the estate at Wycombe.

And to Elfwin, his sister's son, [he gives] the estate at Froxfield.

And, finally, I give to my wife, Elfswith, if she outlives me, all the other land and estates that I leave, provided that she maintain them as I trust she will. And if she keeps God most earnestly in mind, and is zealous for our souls, she is to have the estate at Batcombe for as long as she lives, and after her death it is to pass into the possession of our son, Elfward, if he is still alive, and if not, then it shall go to my brothers for as long as they may live, and after their death it shall belong to Glastonbury [Abbey] for the sake of our father, and our mother, and all of us.

*One "hide" equals 120 acres.
†One "pound" equals 240 pennies (pence) or 20 shillings.

And I wish that every man enslaved for the commission of crimes, on each of the estates which I have bequeathed to my friends, shall be set free.

And the king's permission for the making of this will has been witnessed by Edthelfryth, the king's wife, and Bishop Ethelwold, and Ealdorman Elhere, and Ealdorman Athelwine, and Abbot Escwig.

ETHELFLEDA'S WILL

c. 975-991

This is Ethelfleda's will.* First: I give my lord the estate• at Lambourn, and those at Cholsey and at Reading, and four bracelets worth two hundred gold mancus• coins, and four rich robes, and four cups, and four bowls, and four horses. And I pray to my dear lord, for the love of God, that my will may be upheld and validated, and as God is my witness I have made no other.

And I give the estate at Damerham to the town of Glastonbury, for the sake of King Edmund's soul, and for my soul. And I give the estate at Ham to Christ's church in the town of Canterbury, for King Edmund's soul, and for my soul. And I give the estate at Woodham to Ealdorman• Byrtnoth and to my sister, for as long as they live, and after their death to Saint Mary's church at Barking. And I give the estate at Hadham to Ealdorman Byrtnoth and to my sister, for as long as they live, and after their death to Saint Paul's, in London, as property of the bishopric. And I give the estate at Ditton to [the monastery of] Ely [and] to Saint Etheldreda and to her sisters.† And I give the two estates at Cockfield and at Chelsworth to Ealdorman Byrtnoth and to my sister, for as long as they live, and after their death to Saint Edmund's holy site at Bedericesworth. And I give the estate at Fingringhoe to Ealdorman Byrtnoth and to my sister, for as long as they live, and after their death to Saint Peter's church at Mersea. And I give the estate at Polstead to Ealdorman Byrtnoth and to my sister, for as long as they live, and after their death to [the town of] Stoke. And after my death I give the estate at Withermarsh

---

*Daughter of Ealdorman Elfgar, and second wife of King Edmund; after Edmund's death, she married Ealdorman Ethelstan.

†Saint Etheldreda founded the convent; the word *sisters* indicates the nuns of this convent.

to Stoke. And I give Ealdorman Byrtnoth and my sister the estate
at Stratford, for as long as they live, and after their death I give it to
Stoke. And after the deaths of the ealdorman and my sister I give
Lavenham to Stoke. And after the deaths of the ealdorman and my
sister I give the estate at Baldon to Stoke. And after my death, and
the deaths of Ealdorman Byrtnoth and my sister, I give the estates
at Peldon and at Mersea and at Greenstead to Stoke. And I give the
estate at Elmsett to Ealdorman Byrtnoth and to my sister, for as long
as they live, and after their death I give it to Edmund.* And after my
death I give the single hide† at Thorpe to [the town of] Hadleigh, for
my soul and for the souls of my ancestors.

And after my death I give the ten hides at Wickford to my kins-
man, Sibriht. And after my death I give my steward, Ecgwine, the
four hides at Hadham, exactly as they used to be in the old days. And
after my death I give my servant Brihtwold two hides [of land] in
Donyland. And after my death I give my priest Elfwold two hides [of
land] in Donyland. And after my death I give my priest Ethelmær two
hides [of land] in Donyland. And after my death I give my kinsman
Elfgeat two hides [of land] in Donyland. And after my death I give
my kinswoman Crawe the estate at Waldingfield.

And I wish half the men in every village and town be freed, for the
sake of my soul. And that half the livestock I own, in each town and
village, be distributed, for the sake of my soul.

WULFWARU'S WILL

c. 984–1016

I, Wulfwaru,‡ beg of my beloved lord, King Ethelred, that he,
for the sake of charity, will allow me to make my will. Dear lord, I
declare, here in this document, what I give to Saint Peter's monastery
in Bath, for my poor soul and for [the souls of] my ancestors, from
whom my lands and all I own came to me. Accordingly, I give

---

*Unknown.

†See note to Ealdorman Elfheah's will, above.

‡A woman, and unknown. One of her son's names alliterates with /w/, but
the other alliterates differently (in Old English, all vowels alliterate with all other
vowels), indicating that she probably married twice.

that holy place a bracelet worth sixty gold mancus• coins, and a
bowl worth two and a half pounds, and two gold crucifixes, and
the vestments for saying Mass, along with everything thereunto
belonging, and the best mantle I have, and bedclothes, together with
bed curtains and bedcovering, along with everything thereunto be-
longing. And I give Abbot Elfhere the estate• at Freshford, together
with the crops grown there, and the people, and all the profits earned.

And I give to Wulfmar, my oldest son, the estate at Claverton,
together with the crops grown there, and the people, and all the
profits earned; and the estate at Compton, together with the crops
grown there, and the people, and all the profits earned; and I give
him half the estate at Butcombe, together with the crops grown
there, and the people, and all the profits earned, with the other half to
go to Alfware, my younger daughter, together with the crops grown
there, and the people, and all the profits earned; and they are to share
the main house between them as fairly and justly as they can, so that
each may have an equal portion.

And to Elfwine, my younger son, I give the estate at Leigh,
together with the crops grown there, and the people, and all the
profits earned. And [I give him]the estate at Holton, together with
the crops grown there, and the people, and all the profits earned. And
[I give him] the estate at Hogston, together with the crops grown
there, and the people, and all the profits earned, and thirty gold
mancus coins.

And I give to Gode, my elder daughter, the estate at Winford,
together with all the crops grown there, and the people, and the
profits earned, and two cups worth four pounds, and a headband
worth thirty gold mancus coins, and two brooches, and one full set of
women's clothing. And I give to Alfware, my younger daughter, all
the remaining women's clothing.

And to my son, Wulfmar, and to my second son, Elfwine, and to
my daughter, Alfware, I give each of the three of them two cups of
good value. And I give my son Wulfmar a hall tapestry and one set of
bedclothes. And to my second son, Elfwine, I give one piece of hall
tapestry, and one room tapestry, together with a tablecloth and all the
table napkins thereunto belonging.

And I give to my four servants—Alfmer, Alfweard, Wulfric, and

Wulfstan—a headband worth twenty gold mancus coins. And I give to all my women-servants, in common, a good, well-decorated chest.*

And I wish that all my heirs furnish to the monastery at Bath ten freedmen, ten from the east, and ten from the west,† and all of the heirs together are to furnish said monastery, till the end of time, as good a yearly food rent as they are able, as and when all of them together think it most appropriate. Whoever among them do this will have God's favor and mercy, and mine. And whoever among them will not do this will have to deal with the Most High, He Who is the True God and created and brought into existence the entire creation.

EALDORMAN ETHELWOLD'S WILL

c. 946–947

It is hereby declared that King Edward [the Elder, reigned 940–946,] gives the estate• at Wiley, comprising twelve hides, for the furnishing of clothing for the community of the old monastery [at Winchester].

Ealdorman• Ethelwold hereby declares to his beloved sovereign lord, King Edward, my wishes concerning the property that belongs to me.

First, for the furnishing of clothing for the community, [I give] the estate at Wiley, comprising twelve hides, to God and to the holy bishopric at Winchester, and to the bishop and the members of the holy community there, so that they may keep me in their prayers, just as I expect of them.

And [I give] my weapons and armor to the king:‡ four swords, and four spears, and four shields, and four bracelets, and a hundred and twenty-two mancus• coins, plus eighty-two more, and four horses, and two silver cups.

And to my brother Edric I give the estates at Ogbourne and at

---

*The word *castenere* can also mean a cabinet.

†Perhaps a form of manumission: the meaning is uncertain.

‡This is the feudal tribute known as "heriot," which originally applied, according to A. J. Wyatt, "to the arms given to a tenant by his lord and surrendered at his death."

Ashdown and at Cheam and at Washington. And to my brother
Ethelstan I give the estates at Broadwater and at Newton. And to
Elfsige, my brother's son, [I give] the estate at Carcel, and to Elfstan,
my brother's son, the estate at Kingsclere.

And I wish that all the property I have leased may be distributed,
for the sake of my soul, exactly as I have now informed my friends
that it should be.

OLD ENGLISH LAWS

The Germanic legal code began as an oral system, but after his
conversion by Saint Augustine of Canterbury, King Ethelberht of
Kent (560–617) instituted a tradition of legal writing in English.
King Alfred inherited this tradition, and his laws were recorded in
manuscript soon after their completion. Anglo-Saxon kings did not
frame new laws but conveyed and interpreted the received codes and
customs of their time. Alfred's laws, for example, incorporate the laws
of King Ine (688–725). Alfred views law as God's ordinance, and he
quotes from Moses and the apostles, as well as such predecessors as
King Ine. He viewed the chief task of the legislator as bringing the
body of customary law into line with Christian practices. Alfred's
laws demonstrate great fairness toward all his people, including "a
peasant who has been disgraced."

The brief text that is here entitled "Judgment by Ordeal" (and is
called "Trial by Ordeal" by modern editors) is found in a twelfth-
century manuscript. Lawsuits were a social matter: a defendant
made an oath and was assisted by oath-helpers who testified to his
innocence. Under some circumstances, the accused might be required
to undergo an ordeal, witnessed by people on each side.

One segment of Alfred's laws includes his treaty with King Guth-
rum of Denmark. The date of the treaty is uncertain, although the
text mentions that Guthrum resides in East Anglia, which means
that it must have been entered into after 880 but before Guthrum's
death in 890. Guthrum's defeat and subsequent submission to Alfred
marked a turning point in England's history, and the treaty provides
further demonstration of Alfred's fairness, even to his enemies.

KING ALFRED'S LAWS: EXCERPTS

1. *Concerning oaths, covenants, pledges, and contracts.* The first thing we teach is that it is essential for every man to carefully carry out his oaths and promises. Should anyone be wrongfully compelled to make any such covenant—whether it be to commit treason to a lord or the furtherance of any unlawful act—then it would be better to break than fulfill such an oath. But if he has sworn to do what it is right that he do and breaks that pledge, let him humbly give his weapons and his property to his friends to hold, and be confined for forty nights in the king's prison, to suffer there as the bishop may direct and to be fed by his kinsmen if he himself has no food. Should he be without kin or without food, then the king's sheriff shall feed him. Should force be required, and he be chained, since otherwise he will not [go to jail], then he shall surrender his weapons and his property. Should anyone then kill him, no wergeld• for such a death shall be paid. Should he flee from jail before his time is up and be recaptured, he shall lie in jail for forty [more] nights, as he was supposed to in the first instance. If he makes good his escape, he shall be outlawed and excommunicated from all of Christ's churches. If anyone has provided bail for him, then that surety shall be paid as the law may prescribe, and penance for that oath-breaking shall be performed as his confessor shall direct.

32. *Concerning slander.* Should a man be guilty of slander, and it be proven against him, he shall be punished by nothing less than the cutting off of his tongue, and he shall not redeem himself from that punishment by the payment of a sum smaller than the wergeld to be paid for the taking of that man's life.

35. *Concerning tying up a peasant.* Should a peasant be tied up, and that peasant be innocent, a payment of ten shillings shall be made. If the peasant has been beaten, the payment shall be twenty shillings. If the peasant has been put in prison, or into the stocks,* the payment shall be thirty shillings. If the peasant has been disgraced by having his hair cropped, the payment shall be ten shillings. If the peasant

*A device for restraining someone by the ankles and sometimes also by the wrists.

has been tonsured like a priest, the payment shall be thirty shillings. If the peasant's beard has been cut off, the payment shall be twenty shillings. If the peasant is first tied up and then sheared like a priest, the payment shall be sixty shillings.

46. *Concerning cutting off an ear.* If a man cut another's ear off, he shall pay thirty shillings. If hearing is lost, and the man be deaf, the payment shall be sixty shillings.

JUDGMENT BY ORDEAL

On Incendiaries and Murderers We have declared that in the case of an incendiary or a murderer, the oath for such a man shall be increased threefold, and the weight of iron to be carried in the ordeal* shall be increased to three pounds, and the accused man shall come to the ordeal, and the accuser shall have the choice whether it be ordeal by water or ordeal by iron, as he may prefer. If the accused cannot make the required oath, and is thereby [proven] guilty, it shall be for the chief men of that town to decide whether he shall be kept alive.

Statute Concerning Hot Iron and Water 1. And, concerning the ordeal, we proclaim that, as ordered by God and the archbishop and all the bishops, no man shall be allowed to enter the church, once the fire required for the ordeal has been brought therein, except the priest and he who is to undergo the ordeal, and from the post† to the mark‡ nine feet shall be measured, according to the feet of the man undergoing the ordeal.

---

*Bosworth and Toller's *Anglo-Saxon Dictionary* explains the judicial ordeal as follows: "After the fire to be used in heating was carried into the church, none were to enter but the priest and the accused. When the iron was hot or the water boiled, two men for the accused, two for the accuser, were admitted, to see that the proceedings were fairly conducted. When the hot water was employed . . . the hand was plunged in up to the wrist, [and] if of threefold, up to the elbow. When the hot iron was used, a weight of one pound or of three pounds, according to the case, had to be carried nine feet. The hand was then sealed up, and its condition, when unwrapped at the end of three days, determined the guilt or innocence of the accused."

† Where the heated iron or water was placed.

‡ To which the heated iron had to be carried.

2.* And if it is by water, it shall be heated until it is hot enough to boil, no matter whether the cooking vessel be iron or brass, lead or clay.

3. And if it is a simple† accusation, the hand that reaches for the stone must go in up to the wrist, and if it be threefold, then it [must go] to the elbow.

4. And when the ordeal has been made ready, then two men on each side shall go in [to the church], and they must be unanimously agreed that it is as hot as we have earlier specified.

5. And [after that] an equal number of men from each side shall go in [to the church], and stand along the two sides of the church, and every one of these men shall have been fasting, and shall have refrained from their wives that night, and the priest shall sprinkle holy water over them all, and they shall each of them taste the holy water, and all of them shall kiss the book and the symbol of Christ's crucifixion, and no one shall feed or fan the fire once this consecration has begun, and the iron shall be permitted to lie there, on the embers, until final prayers, after which it shall be placed on the post, and no one in the church shall say any other word except that they shall earnestly pray to Almighty God that the indisputable truth be made known.

6. And when the accused has gone to the ordeal, his hand shall be wrapped, and the wrapping sealed, and after three days it shall be inspected to see whether it is completely clear‡ [or discolored], there inside the seal.

7. And if anyone breaks this statute, the ordeal shall be declared null and void, and the law-breaker shall pay a fine of one hundred and twenty shillings to the king.

---

*Renumbered from the Old English text edited by F. L. Attenborough, in which the numeral "1" is followed by six subsections, numbered from one to six.

†As in "singular; just one; lowest level."

‡The word *claene,* significantly, can also mean "innocent."

KING ALFRED'S TREATY WITH
KING GUTHRUM OF DENMARK

c. 880

This is the truce-agreement that King Alfred and King Guthrum
and the Witan• of the entire English people, and all the people of
East Anglia, have all agreed upon and solemnized with oaths, for
themselves and for their descendants, whether born or unborn, who
are concerned with both God's mercy and ours.

1. First: as to our boundaries: as far as the Thames, and then up the
Lea, and along the Lea to its source, then in a straight line to Bedford,
and then up the Ouse to Watling Street.

2. Should anyone be killed, no matter whether he be English or
Danish, [the wergeld•] shall be eight half-marks of pure gold, with
the exception of [a] peasant working rented land and [b] Danish
freedmen, who shall both be valued equally: two hundred shillings
for either.

3. And if anyone accuses a king's thane• of murder, and the accused
venture to acquit himself, he shall do so by [the sworn testimony of]
twelve royal courtiers. But if the accused should be of lower status
than a king's courtier, he shall acquit himself by [the sworn testimony
of] eleven of the same status as himself, together with one royal
courtier. And this shall be applicable in any legal action involving a
sum greater than four mancus• coins. And if the accused does not
defend himself against the accusation, he must make a payment equal
to three times what he would otherwise be obliged to pay.

4. And every man must be sure he knows the man who gives him
a guarantee, when he buys slaves or horses or oxen.

5. And we have all declared, on the day when [these] oaths were
sworn, that neither slaves nor freedmen shall be allowed to travel
over to the Danish army without permission, nor shall any of them
come over to us. But if it happens that any Dane should need to do
any business with us, or we with them, whether in cattle or in other
goods, such commerce shall be permitted as follows: namely, that
hostages• or other pledges shall be given to ensure peace and clearly
to demonstrate that straightforward transactions are intended.

Religious Prose

Anglo-Saxon prose flourished in the late ninth century under King Alfred (reigned 871–899). When Alfred began his educational program to make every free-born boy literate in English, he was less concerned to reproduce Latin texts than to produce books that would give his subjects a practical and liberal education. Alfred expanded his sources, using similes to clarify abstract arguments. And because he drew these similes from his own experiences, they provide insights into his character and time. Alfred's version of Augustine's *Soliloquies,* for example, contains the earliest extant definition of *bocland,* "entailed• estate•," a word he also uses in his will.

Alfred's successors did not maintain the standards of literacy he had prized so highly. It was not until the peaceful reign of Alfred's great-grandson Edgar (reigned 959–975) that literacy again flourished. This second flowering of literature was dominated by two great writers in the vernacular, Aelfric and Wulfstan, but works by numerous anonymous authors also survive. Two collections of homilies, the *Blickling Homilies* and the *Vercelli Book Homilies* (accompanying the four poems of the Vercelli MS), along with many other works, such as the *Harrowing of Hell,* attest to the liveliness of intellectual activity in this period.

KING ALFRED'S PREFACE TO GREGORY'S *DIALOGUES*

The Dialogues *were translated by Bishop Wefrith of Worcester for Alfred be-*
tween his ascension to the throne and the early 890s. The Dialogues *are filled*
with stories both edifying and escapist, narrating the wonders done by God
and the miracles of the saints. Gregory (pope, 590–604) as a pope enmeshed in
secular affairs must have been of particular interest to Alfred, king of a wartorn
land. In this brief preface, Alfred speaks of the need to study "divine and
spiritual law" while surrounded by "earthly concerns." He praises his "true and
faithful friends" for providing the "precepts and teachings" for him to study.

I, Alfred, endowed by the grace of Christ with the high favor of
royal dignity, do most emphatically understand (as through the read-
ing and explanation of holy books I have often heard) that the One
God has given us an immensity of worldly honors. It is desperately
urgent, at times, in the midst of all these earthly concerns, that we
soothe and relieve our minds, bending them to the consideration of
divine and spiritual law, and I therefore desired, and urged my true
and faithful friends, that from the books of God they would write
out for me the following precepts and teachings, which concern the
way of life and the miracles of sanctified men, so that I, by means of
these admonitions and exhortations, and this holy passion, might be
strengthened in my mind and enabled, sometimes, here among all
my earthly troubles and confusions, to study heavenly matters. Truly,
we are now able for the first time to hear how the blessed, Apostolic
Saint Gregory spoke to his deacon, whose name was Peter, about the
lives and practices of sanctified men, teaching and inspiring all those
who seek to do the will of God, for he spoke of himself, in writing
these words, and this is what he said.

AELFRIC'S SERMON FOR DECEMBER 27, ON THE
ASSUMPTION OF SAINT JOHN THE APOSTLE

Aelfric (c. 955–1020) composed two volumes known as the Catholic Homilies
as well as a volume of Lives of the Saints. *Although he wrote the* Catholic
Homilies *for his own use, he later revised them for more general distribution.*
The doctrine Aelfric expresses is straightforward and orthodox, in keeping with
the basic tenets of the Catholic church. He repeatedly deals with such themes
as God the Creator, the Trinity, the life and works of Christ, and redemption.

One of Aelfric's central concerns was to teach those who in turn would be instructing the laity.

The Sermon for December 27 is the fourth homily of the First Series of Catholic Homilies *and is a free adaptation of parts of the apocryphal Acts of John.* This homily is one of Aelfric's earliest works, and it has been praised for its simple and dignified style. Influenced by the emphasis on monasticism that characterized the Benedictine Reform movement, Aelfric depicts the Apostle John as famous for "the purity of his incorruptible chastity." John is gentle and kind, as is shown by his resurrection of the widow Drusiana, but he is also firm. When Atticus and Eugenius abandon their faith for earthly treasure, John teaches them that earthly riches have little value, and, through this narrative, Aelfric also teaches his audience.*

John the Evangelist, dearly beloved of Christ, was on this day, through God's dispensation, taken to the joys of the kingdom of Heaven. He was the son of Christ's maternal aunt, and Christ felt a very special love for him, not so much because they were closely related as for the purity of his incorruptible chastity, which had been appointed by God, and he kept this chastity forever unspotted. We read in historical accounts that he had intended to marry, and Christ had been invited to the wedding. But, as it happened, there was no wine for the wedding. So Our Lord and Savior told the servingmen to fill six stone vessels with clear water, and His blessing turned that water into noble wine. This was the first public miracle He worked, in His human form. And John was so inspired by this miracle that he immediately left his still virginal bride, and forever after followed Our Lord, and was dearly beloved by Him because he had freed himself from the desires of the flesh. Indeed, Our Lord and Savior entrusted His mother to this beloved disciple when, hanging on the Cross, He redeemed mankind, so that John's pure life could take care of the holy Virgin, Mary, and so she could continue in the service of her sister's son.

Some time later, after Christ's ascension to Heaven, a cruel and barbarous emperor named Domitian succeeded Nero to the Roman throne, and he was a persecutor of Christians. He ordered a great vat filled with boiling oil, and commanded that the celebrated Evangelist

---

*For Aelfric's source, see J. K. Elliott, *The Apocryphal New Testament* (Oxford: Clarendon Press, 1993), 311–345.

be hurled in, but God's protection kept him unharmed by that hot bath. Afterward, when the bloodthirsty emperor was unable to keep the blessed Apostle from preaching, he had him banished to a tiny island called Patmos, intending that he would die there, of the pangs of starvation. But the Almighty Saviour did not abandon His beloved Apostle, revealing to him, in his exile, all that which was to come, which John then wrote down in the book named THE APOCALYPSE, and in that very same year the cruel Domitian was killed at the hands of his own counselors, who unanimously declared that all Domitian's laws and statutes were null and void. And then Nerva, a truly good and virtuous man, was chosen as emperor. He allowed the Apostle to return, in great dignity and honor, though he had been most scornfully sent into exile. Men and women alike came running to him, most joyfully, saying: "Blessed is he who comes in God's name."

As the Apostle John arrived in the city of Ephesus, men came toward him, carrying to its burial the corpse of a widow; her name was Drusiana. She was a true believer and a great giver of alms to the poor, and these needy people, whom she had most bountifully fed, were following after the corpse, sorrowing and weeping. Then the Apostle told them to put down the bier, and said: "My Lord, Christ Our Savior! Rise up, Drusiana—arise, and return home, and prepare a meal for us at your house." And Drusiana rose up, just as if awakened from sleep, and, attentive to the Apostle's command, went back to her home.

The next day, as the Apostle was walking down the street, he saw a certain scholar and wise man leading along two brothers, who had turned all their parents' wealth and treasures into precious gems, which they intended to crush to dust in full public view, to show how utterly they despised worldly riches. It was quite customary, at that time, for those who intended to diligently study the worldly sciences to turn all their property into gemstones and then smash them to bits or else into a bar of gold, which they would cast into the sea, for fear that the very contemplation of that wealth would interfere with their study. Then the Apostle called to the wise man, whose name was Graton, and said, "How foolish to despise worldly wealth, in order to win men's praise, and still to be condemned by God, at the Last Judgment, to eternal punishment. What use is a cure that cannot heal the sick? And so, too, is that learning empty and useless, which does not heal the sins and evil ways of the soul. Truly, Christ my teacher once taught a young man who longed for eternal life with these words: if he wished to achieve perfection, let him sell his riches, and give all they were worth to the poor, and afterwards he would have his treasure in Heaven, and in addition would enjoy life eternal." Then Graton, the wise man, answered him: "These gemstones will be crushed in empty arrogance, but if your teacher is indeed the true God, let the pieces be put back together again, so their worth may benefit the poor." So John gathered up the pieces of gemstone and cast his eyes toward Heaven, and said as follows: "My Lord and Savior, nothing is too difficult for You. You restored this broken world on behalf of Your faithful, by the sign of the Holy Cross. Now restore these precious gems, by Your angels' hands, so that these ignorant men can come to know Your might, and believe in You." Lo and behold: suddenly, the gemstones were whole once more, and not a sign that they had just been broken to little pieces could be seen. Then the wise man, Graton, and the two young brothers with him, fell at John's feet, and believed in God. Then the Apostle baptized Graton, and all his family, and he began to publicly preach God's faith. And the two brothers, Atticus and Eugenius, gave all their gemstones, and all the rest of their wealth, to the poor and needy, and followed after the Apostle, and many, many other believers joined with them.

And then it happened, once, that the Apostle came to the city of Pergamus, where the two brothers just mentioned used to live, and there the two young men saw their very own servants decked out in precious purple cloth, resplendent with worldly splendor. Then the devil's arrows pierced them through and through and left them sorrowing that they had to go about, wrapped in a single miserable cloak, while their servants were all glittering and gleaming in worldly splendor. Understanding the devil's lying tricks, the Apostle said, "I see how your hearts have changed, and your appearance, because you have given all your wealth to the poor, following the teaching of my Lord. Now go to the wood, and cut yourselves a load of sticks, and bring them to me." They did as he directed, and he blessed the green sticks, in God's name, and they were turned into red gold. And then the Apostle John said, "Now go to the seashore, and bring me pebbles." Which they did, and by the power and glory of God he

blessed the stones, and they were turned to precious gems. And then
the Apostle said, "Go to the smiths, and have them test this gold and
these gemstones." So they went, and then they came back, saying,
"All the goldsmiths say they've never seen such pure gold, nor any so
red, and the jewelers, too, say they've never encountered such pre-
cious gems." Then the Apostle said to them, "Take this gold, and these
gems, and go buy land for yourselves, now that you've surrendered
your heavenly wealth. Buy yourselves rich purple garments, so that,
for a little while, you can shine like roses, and as quickly wither away.
Flourish and be rich, for a while, so you be poor forever. What? Can't
the Almighty Ruler let His servants prosper in the sight of the world,
rolling in riches, and shining incomparably bright? But He has cre-
ated a battle for His believers' souls, letting them believe so that those
who will, in His name, despise all transitory wealth, may possess eter-
nal wealth. You have healed the sick, in our Savior's name; you have
driven out devils; you gave sight to the blind; there is no disease you
could not cure. Ah, but now these gifts have been taken from you,
and you, who were great and strong, have become poor miserable
wretches. The devils were so terrified of you that, at your very word,
they abandoned those of whom they had taken possession; now you
yourselves are terrified of devils. Heavenly wealth belongs to all of us.
We were all born naked, and naked we all leave. The sun's brilliance,
and the moon's light, and that of the stars, belong to us all, high and
low alike. Rain showers, and church doors, and baptism, and the for-
giveness of sin, and partaking of the holy Eucharist•, and the blessing
of God's grace, belong to us all, the poor and the rich. But the miser-
able miser wants still more than the abundance he already has, though
his overflowing plenty does not let him live free of anxiety and care.
The miser has only one body, but a great many clothes; he possesses
one belly, but a thousand men's nourishment; and truly, what this
vice of avarice will not let him give to anyone else, he hoards away,
but does not know for whom, for as the prophet has said, 'Every man
who hoards, but does not know for whom he is gathering and keep-
ing these things, is afflicted and troubled.' In truth, he is not master of
what he owns, since he cannot share or spend it; rather, he is the ser-
vant of his wealth, perpetually enslaved to it; and then, moreover, his
body grows ill and weak, so he cannot enjoy either food or drink. He
worries, day and night, that he can hold on to his money; greedily,

he tends to his business, and the profit it brings him—collecting his rents, watching over his houses; he despoils the poor, pursuing his desires and his delights; and then, suddenly, he leaves this world, naked and condemned, carrying with him only his sins; and therefore he will surely suffer eternal torment."

And lo! as the Apostle was thus preaching, a certain widow came, carrying her son's body to be buried; he had been married thirty days earlier. His sorrowing mother, along with the wailing mourners, threw herself at the Apostle's feet, begging that, in God's name, he would raise up her son, as he had the widow Drusiana. Then John, taking pity on the grief of the mother and all the mourners, threw himself to the ground and lay there a long time, praying, and finally stood up, and with his hands raised high prayed, again for a long time. And when he had done this three times, he directed them to unwind the shroud from the dead body, and said, "Oh, young man, you who have through fleshly desire so soon lost your soul! Oh, young man, you who never knew your Creator, nor knew the Savior of all men—who never knew your one true friend, and thus have been carried off by the worst of all fiends! Now I have poured out my tears, and prayed most earnestly on your behalf, on account of your ignorance, rise from the dead, and tell these two brothers, Atticus and Eugenius, what immense glory they have given up, and what punishment they have earned!" At these words the young man, whose name was Stacteus, rose from the dead, and fell at John's feet, and began to rebuke the two brothers who had been corrupted, saying to them, "I saw the angels who were watching over you, and how sadly they were weeping, and I saw the accursed demon exulting in your ruin. The kingdom of Heaven had been made ready for you, and shining houses had been filled with food and drink, and with eternal light. You have recklessly lost all this, and what you have gotten for yourselves is dark dwelling-places filled with serpents and with crackling flames, filled with indescribable torments and a horrible, fetid stench, and the groaning and wailing never stops, day and night. So pray to this Apostle of God, your teacher, deep in your heart, that he lift you out of this eternal perdition, just as he has raised me from death, and that he bring your souls, now crossed out of the pages of life's book, back into God's mercy and grace."

And then this young man, Stacteus, who had risen from death, and the two brothers with him, fell at John's feet, as did all the people there, one and all praying that he would intercede on their behalf with God. And the Apostle directed the two brothers that they do penitence for thirty days, making amends to God, and during that time should most earnestly pray that the sticks of gold might be transformed back into the ordinary wood they had been before and the gemstones become once again worthless pebbles. But when, after thirty days, their prayers had not been able to transform the gold and jewels back to their former state, they came crying to the Apostle, saying, "You have always preached mercy and compassion, and that men should be merciful to one another, and yet if men are merciful to their fellows, how much more will God be merciful and compassionate to men, for He made them! The sin we committed, with greedy eyes, we now most tearfully repent." And the Apostle replied, "Take the sticks back to the woods, and the pebbles to the seashore: they will be turned back into what they were." When they had done this, God's grace was restored to them, and they were able to drive out devils, and heal the blind and the sick, and performed an abundance of miracles in God's name, exactly as they had done before.

And then the Apostle brought all of Asia, which is considered to contain half the people in the whole world, to God, and he wrote the fourth book of Christ, which is primarily concerned with His divinity. The other three Evangelists — Matthew, Mark, and Luke — were more concerned with His human state. For there began to be heretics in God's congregations, who said that Christ had not existed until He was born of Mary. Then the bishops of all the dioceses begged the holy Apostle to write the fourth book and stamp out the heretics' rashness. So John ordered that there be a general fast of three days, and after that fast he was so inspired by the spirit of God that the lofty sublimity of his mind towered above even that of all God's angels, and that of all created beings, and he began the writing of the fourth book of the Gospel with these words "In principio erat uerbum, et uerbum erat apud Deum, et Deus erat uerbum, et reliqua" — or, as we say in English, "In the beginning was the Word, and that Word was with God, and that Word was God; this was in the beginning, with God; for all things are created by Him, and nothing created has not been made by Him." And so he continued, through the writing of the whole Gospel, making Christ's divinity known, how He was created, eternally, by His Father, without any beginning, and He rules with God, together with the Holy Ghost, forever and ever. He wrote very little about Christ's human state, since the other three Evangelists had more than sufficiently dealt with that subject in what they had written.

Now it came to pass that those who worshiped idols and who still did not believe in God declared that they would force the Apostle into their heathen• religion. And the Apostle said to the heathens, "Come, all of you together, to God's church, and then call out to all your gods that, with their power and might, the church be leveled to the ground—and then I will submit to your heathen worship. But if your gods are not strong enough to destroy God's church, I will destroy your temple, through the might of Almighty God, and I will crush your idol, and then it will be plain that you are to forswear your errors and believe in the one true God, for He alone is Almighty." The heathens agreed to this proposal, and with kind and gentle words John invited them to leave their temple and go outside, and then in a loud, clear voice, right in front of them all, he called, "In the name of God, let this temple fall down, together with all the idols residing inside it, so that these multitudes may know that this worshiping of idols is a cult of the devil." And lo, the temple suddenly fell to the ground, and all its idols were turned to dust. And that very same day twelve thousand heathens were converted to belief in Christ and were hallowed by being baptized.

And still the chief of the idol worshipers, from sheer depraved perversity, refused to accept Christ, saying that he would believe only if John were to drink poison and by the might of God was able to survive it. So the Apostle said, "You may give me poison to drink, but by God's name it will not hurt me." And Aristodemus, the heathen, said, "First, watch while someone else drinks it, and is immediately killed, so that your heart, at least, will tremble at this death-bearing drink." John answered, "If you are prepared to believe in God, I will take this drink without the slightest fear." Then Aristodemus hurried to the high sheriff and took two thieves from his prison, and, in John's presence, and in front of everyone, gave them the poison, and as soon as they drank it, they died. And then the heathen gave the poison-filled drink to the Apostle, and he made the sign of the cross over his mouth, and armed his whole body in the same manner, and exorcised the poison in God's name, and then confidently drank every drop of it. Aristodemus and the others watched the Apostle for three days and saw that his face remained calm and cheerful, utterly without any sign of fear or pallor, and they all cried, "There is only one God, and it is the God John worships!" But the heathen said to the Apostle, "And still I doubt. But if you raise these criminals from the dead, in the name of your God, then my heart will be freed of every doubt." So John said, "Aristodemus, take my coat, and put it over these men's corpses, and say, 'The Apostle of Christ Our Savior sends me to you, so that you can rise from the dead in His name, and so that all other men may know that both death and life serve my Savior.'" So Aristodemus took the Apostle's coat and laid it over the two dead men, and at once they rose up, whole and alive. And when the idol worshiper saw that, he threw himself at John's feet, and then went to the high sheriff and, in a loud voice, told him of these miracles. And then they both went to the Apostle, begging for his forgiveness. And the Apostle told them to fast for seven nights, after which he baptized them, and after their baptism they overthrew all their idols, and with their kinsmen's help, and using all the skills they possessed, they built God a splendid church in the Apostle's honor.

When the Apostle was ninety-nine years old, Christ Our Lord appeared to him, together with the other Apostles He had already taken out of this life, and said, "John, come to me. It is time that you and your brethren feast at my table." So John arose and walked toward the Savior, but He said, "You will come to me on Sunday, the day of my Resurrection." And having spoken these words, Our Lord returned to Heaven. The Apostle was wonderfully happy at this promise and rose early, that Sunday morning, and came to church and, from the crowing of the cock until nine in the morning, preached God's law to the people, and sang Mass to them, and told them that the Savior had called him to come to Heaven that day. He ordered his grave dug behind the altar and the earth taken away. And then, alive as he was, he went down into his grave and, stretching his hands up toward God, called out, "My Lord Christ, I thank You for having invited me to Your feast, for You know that was what I wanted with all my heart. I have prayed to You, often, to let me come to You, but You said I was to wait, so that I might gather more people to You. You have kept my body free of all corruption, and Your light has always filled my soul, and You have never forsaken me. You put Your words of truth into my mouth, and I have written down the teachings I heard You speak, and the wonders I saw You work. Now I deliver Your children to You, oh Lord—the congregations which Your Virgin Mother acquired in Your name, by means of baptism and the Holy Ghost. Take me, now, to my brethren, together with whom You came and invited me to You. Let the gate of life open toward me, that the princes of darkness may never find me. You are Christ, Son of the Living God, who because Your Father so desired it saved the world and sent us the Holy Ghost. We praise You, and we thank You for Your many goodnesses through all eternity. Amen."

After this prayer a heavenly light appeared above the Apostle, shining so brightly in the grave that no man's eyes could stand to look at it, and in the midst of that light he surrendered his spirit to the Lord, who had called him to His kingdom. He went from this earthly life, and from the pain and affliction of death, exactly as he had always been immune from all bodily corruption. Indeed, his grave was afterward found to be filled with manna from Heaven, that heavenly food which, as they journeyed through the wilderness, for forty years fed the people of Israel. And this was the holy nourishment that was found in John's grave, and nothing else, and to this day that same holy nourishment can be found growing there. Many signs and wonders have appeared there, and many sick people have been healed and freed from all dangers and disasters, by means of the Apostle's intercession. Our Lord Christ granted him this, He who, with the Father and the Holy Ghost, is glory and honor forever without end.

AELFRIC'S PREFACE TO HIS TRANSLATION OF GENESIS

The extant biblical texts in Old English consist of a translation of and commentary on the Pentateuch, Joshua, and Judges, known collectively as the Old English Heptateuch. *The entire work was once attributed to Aelfric (c. 955–1020), but it seems likely that he is responsible only for part of Genesis, which he translated at the unwelcome but unrefusable request of his patron, Ethelweard. Aelfric stopped part way through Isaac, he tells us, because someone else had already completed the book. Like King Alfred, Aelfric was concerned to translate his Latin original so that it could be understood by a person literate in English but not in Latin. In addition, he expresses his concern with those who will copy his text lest it be "perverted by lying, indifferent copyists." Aelfric indicates that he fears translating the rest of the Old Testament because the unlearned might misunderstand it; were it to remain only in Latin, it would be less subject to misinterpretation. Aelfric also worries that his audience may assume that "the book's whole meaning is enclosed in the simple narrative." One feature of interest to religious and literary scholars is Aelfric's outline of the way Old Testament events prefigured those of the New Testament: "Joseph, who was sold and surrendered into the land of Egypt and who saved the people from great famine, foretold Christ." His "Preface" therefore provided for his Anglo-Saxon audience an introduction to the allegorical and typological way of reading Scripture.*

Aelfric the monk respectfully greets Ealdorman• Ethelweard. You asked me, my lord, that I should translate the book of Genesis from Latin into English. Agreeing to do this for you seemed to me troublesome, so you said I need translate the book only as far as [the story of] Isaac, Abraham's son, and no farther, because someone else had already translated the book from that story to the end.

But it seems to me, my lord, that this is dangerous work for me, or for anyone else, to undertake, because I am afraid that, should some foolish man read this book, or hear it read, he will suppose himself capable of living, here and now, in the era of the New Law,* exactly as our forefathers lived in the days before the Old Law had been ordained, or as men lived under the Law of Moses. I once knew a priest, who was at the time my teacher, and who had the book of Genesis and could understand some Latin; and he declared that the patriarch Jacob had four wives—two sisters and their handmaids. He spoke the truth, certainly, but he did not know—nor as yet did I— what a sharp distinction there is between the Old Law and the New. In the beginning of this world, brothers took their sisters as their wives, and sometimes a father even had children by his own daughter, and in order to increase the population many men had more wives [than one], and in the beginning men were allowed to mate only with their kinswomen. But today, after Christ's coming, anyone who

*That is, the New Testament; the "Old Law" means the Old Testament.

wishes to live as men lived, either before Moses or under the Law of Moses, cannot be a Christian, nor, moreover, is he worthy that any Christian man sit at table and eat with him.

These ignorant priests, should they understand any small part of books written in Latin, immediately think they can be great teachers; yet, nevertheless, they have no comprehension of the spirituality in these books, and that the Old Law was a sign of things to come, or that, after Christ's Incarnation, the New Testament was a fulfillment of all those things, to which the Old Testament had borne witness, about Christ's coming and His chosen ones. Further, they frequently cite Paul and wonder why they may not have a wife, as the Apostle Peter did, and they do not choose to listen or to understand that, before Christ, the blessed Peter lived according to the Law of Moses, and then Christ came to men and began to preach his Holy Gospel, and chose Peter as his first companion; and then Peter at once forsook his wife, and those among the twelve Apostles who had wives also forsook them, as well as everything they owned, and adhered to Christ's teaching, and the New Law, and the chastity that He Himself declared. Priests are assigned the task of teaching lay people. It would be appropriate, now, that they come to understand the spiritual significance of the Old Law, and what Christ Himself, and His Apostles, taught in the New Testament, so that they might fully open the way to God's faith for the people, and set them an example of good works.

We also wish to assert, in advance, that this book is exceedingly difficult to understand in spiritual terms, and we have written no more than the bare narration. The unlearned might think, therefore, that the book's whole meaning is enclosed in the simple narrative; but that is emphatically not the case. The book is entitled "Genesis"— that is, the Book of Creation—because it is [the Bible's] first book, and speaks of the creation of everything (though it does not speak of the creation of the angels). It begins thus: *"In principio creauit deus celum et terram"*—that is, in English, "In the beginning God created heaven and earth." That was truly how it was done, for in the beginning God Almighty created whatever He wished to create. But according to the spiritual meaning, the beginning is Christ, for as He Himself said to the Jews, "I who speak to you am the beginning." It was by means of this beginning that God the Father made heaven and

earth, for He created everything through His Son, who was eternally
born of Him, and possessed the knowledge of the all-knowing
Father.

Thereafter, the book declares, [still] in the first sentence, *"Et spiritus
dei ferebatur super aquas"*—that is, in English, "And God's Spirit went
forth over the waters." God's Spirit is the Holy Ghost, through whom
the Father brought to life all those creatures He had created by means
of His Son, and the Holy Ghost travels through men's hearts and
brings us forgiveness for our sins, first by means of water, in baptism,
and afterward by means of repentance and penitence; and he who
despises this forgiveness, given by the Holy Ghost, has committed an
eternally unforgivable sin. The Holy Trinity is revealed, later in this
book, in God's words, "Let us make man in our likeness." When He
said, "Let *us* make," the Trinity is revealed, [just as] when He said, "In
our likeness," the true oneness of God is revealed: it was not a plural
"in our likeness" which He spoke, but a singular "in our likeness."
Later, three angels came to Abraham, and he spoke to all three of
them as if speaking only to one. And how did Abel's blood cry out
to God except in the same way that every man's sins accuse him to
God, without the need of words? It is through these little things
that we can understand how profound this book is, in its spiritual
significance, although it is written in straightforward, simple words.
And still later, Joseph, who was sold and surrendered into the land
of Egypt and who saved that people from the great famine, foretold
Christ, who was surrendered to death for our sake, and saved us from
the eternal famine of Hell's torments.

That great tabernacle which Moses erected in the desert, with
such wonderful skill, exactly as God Himself had told him to,
foretold God's church, which He Himself established, by means of
His apostles, with many adornments and with joyous rituals. For
[the making of] that building, the people brought gold and silver
and costly jewels and a whole host of glorious things; some also
brought goathair, as God had commanded. The gold symbolized
our faith and the good intentions we are required to bring to God;
the silver represented God's words and the sacred instructions we
need, in order to accomplish His work; the jewels stood for a variety
of the beauties that are in God's people; the goathair symbolized
the unbending repentance men must feel for their sins. People also

brought many cattle to God, to be sacrificed within the tabernacle, as to which the symbolism is exceedingly complex; and it was commanded that the tails of the sacrificial animals should always be whole, in order to symbolize that God wishes us to continue doing good until the very end of our lives: the tail is then offered in the [good] works [we have done].

Since the aforesaid book is, in many places, very tersely and exactly phrased, though exceedingly profound in its spiritual content, and is structured exactly as God Himself gave it to Moses, who wrote it down, we dare not write, in English, any more fully than the Latin has been written, nor change* the order of the words except when Latin and English have different ways of saying the same thing. He who translates Latin, or makes use of it in his teaching, must always be careful to allow English to follow its own syntax,† or else it will read incorrectly to anyone who does not understand Latin syntax. It must also be kept in mind that there were heretics who wanted to utterly reject the Old Law, and there were others who wished to retain the Old Law and reject the New, exactly as the Jews do. But Christ Himself, and His apostles, taught us to keep the Old Law in a spiritual sense and truly to practice the New. God made us with two eyes and two ears, two nostrils and two lips, two hands and two feet, and so, too, He wanted to have two Testaments brought into this world, the Old and the New, because God does as God wills, and He has no counselors or advisers, nor does any man need to ask Him: "Why are You doing this?" We must bend our wills to His commandments, and we are not permitted to bend His commandments to our own desires.

And now I declare that, after this one, I neither dare nor wish to translate any book from Latin into English, and I beg of you, my lord ealdorman, not to ask this of me again, lest I be disrespectful and disobedient to you, or fall into error if I do [as you ask]. May God be eternally merciful to you.

And now I ask you, in God's name, that if anyone wishes to copy this book, he check it very carefully against my original,‡

---

*The word here translated as "change," *awendan,* also means "translate."
†Aelfric writes "þaet Englisc haebbe his agene wisan," "that English has its own [verbal] ordering."
‡The word here translated as "the original" is *þaere bysne,* "the example."

because I will have no control, even if the book is perverted by lying, indifferent copyists, and even though it will then be their responsibility, and not mine: bad copyists do much evil, if they are not willing to correct their mistakes.

SERMO LUPI, THE WOLF'S SERMON

The complete title of this work is Sermo Lupi ad anglos quando maxime persecuti sunt eos, quod fuit anno milesimo XIIII ab incarnatione Domini nostri Jesu Cristi *(The Wolf's sermon to the English at a time when they were especially greatly persecuted [by the Danes], which was in the year 1014 from the incarnation of Our Lord Jesus Christ). The "wolf" (*lupus, *in Latin) is Wulfstan, archbishop of York, 1002–1023, who used "Wolf" as a pen name. While bishop of London (996–1002), Wulfstan developed a reputation as a preacher, especially of eschatological sermons about the coming of Antichrist. The approach of the millennium and the Viking attacks had made such sermons popular.*

At the time Sermo Lupi *was composed, English morale was low. King Ethelred ("noble council"), nicknamed* Unraed *("unadvised"), was an incompetent ruler. Ethelred's reign was marked by social disorder and crime. England faced successive invasions by Viking armies under Olaf Tryggvason of Norway and Swein, king of Denmark. Ethelred's answer was to pay the Vikings to leave, each time awarding them larger sums. Ethelred was defeated by Swein in 1013 and fled to Normandy, returning to England only after Swein's death in 1015. A year later, Ethelred died and Swein's son Cnut became king of England as well as of Denmark and Norway.*

Five manuscripts of the Sermo Lupi *have survived, attesting to its popularity. Wulfstan catalogs the crimes perpetrated in England, and he warns his audience to amend their ways and follow God's laws. He focuses especially on the theme of treachery and disloyalty, providing a contrast to earlier literature, with its emphasis on loyalty.*

Wulfstan's style is marked by frequent use of such acoustical effects as alliteration and rhyme. This translation carefully replicates such effects, as, for example, in the lines "All we have known has been sacking and starvation, burning and bloodshed . . . stealing and slaughter, plague and pestilence." Wulfstan uses little imagery, preferring a starkly realistic style that minces no words when speaking of such subjects as the gang rape of Englishwomen by Danes.

My beloved people, you must recognize the truth: this world is hurrying on and is approaching its end, and the longer it lasts the worse it will be, so that as we near the coming of Antichrist the world must of necessity become very evil indeed. And you must also understand very well that for many years the Devil has greatly deceived this nation, and there has been little faith among men, though there has been a great deal in our words, and there has been far too much injustice in this land, and not very many men have considered, as earnestly as they should, what must be done, but instead, day after day, all across this land, they have committed more and more evil and injustice and violations of the law, for which reason we have endured much injury and suffering. And if we are to have any relief we must merit it, at God's hands, more than we have until now, for we have labored most earnestly to merit the miseries that currently press on us and must labor even harder to deserve any relief at God's hands, if in the future things are to be better. Indeed! We know perfectly well that serious damages can be repaired only by serious remedies, and we cannot simply sprinkle a great fire with a few drops of water if the blaze is somehow to be extinguished. How urgent it is that, from this time on, every man diligently observe all of God's laws and faithfully carry out His commandments.

No man among the heathen• peoples dares to withhold anything, be it small or large, which has been ordained for the worship of idols and false gods, yet in each and every respect we all too frequently withhold that which is owed to God. And among the heathen, no man dares diminish, in any way whatever, the sacrificial offerings brought to their idols, yet we have totally despoiled God's house. And God's servants are everywhere deprived of the respect and protection owed them, yet among the heathen no man dares in any way to mistreat those who serve their idols—as, in these days, God's servants are often mistreated, and in places where Christians ought to uphold God's laws and protect His servants.

I speak the plain truth: and a remedy is required, for in every corner of this land, from one end to the other, God's commandments have been for too long less and less observed, and since the days of King Edgar* secular laws have all fallen into disregard, and sacred

*Edgar the Peaceful (reigned 959–975).

shrines go widely unprotected, and God's houses have been deprived of what has always been due them, as within their four walls they have been stripped of everything that ought to be there, and the men of religion have for too long been treated with deep contempt, and widows illicitly compelled to marry and, in many cases, have been forced into poverty, and poor, entirely innocent men deceived and betrayed, miserably entrapped and sold into distant lands, into the power of strangers, and children barely out of the cradle cruelly and unlawfully enslaved for petty thievery, and the rights of freemen annulled, and the rights of serfs restricted, and the right to seek alms reduced, and—to be as brief as possible—God's laws hated and His teachings despised, for all of which (as it ought not be difficult to see) we have suffered miserably, and for all of which we will as a people (though not everyone realizes it) go on suffering, without God's protection.

Surely it is plain and obvious that, until now, we have broken more often than we have mended, and that this people has experienced so many onslaughts for exactly this reason. For a long time, there has been nothing good, neither at home nor abroad, and all we have known has been sacking and starvation, burning and bloodshed, everywhere and often, and we have been sorely afflicted by stealing and slaughter, plague and pestilence, sickness among our cattle and among ourselves, by vicious words and feelings and exceedingly rapacious deeds, and heavy, unreasonable taxes have oppressed us, and storms have often caused our crops to fail—and all because, we may suppose, for many years all this land has seen, everywhere and among all men, has been injustice and instability. Often, in these days, men offer their kinsmen, and fathers their children, and sometimes even children their own fathers, or one brother another, no more protection than they offer a stranger. No one of us has ordered and directed his life as he should—neither those in holy orders, according to the rules they have vowed to obey, nor laymen, according to the laws of the land. No one of us has tried to be faithful to others, acting justly and lawfully, as he should, but almost all of us have cheated and injured others, both in word and in deed. And, especially, almost all of us have attacked others from behind, with slanderous words—and would do still worse, if he could! Which is why we have, here in our land, many who are untrue both to God and to man, as also we have

in this land many who, in various ways, are untrue to their lords, and
betraying your lord's soul is the worst treachery in this world. But
there is another very great treachery, and that is either to plot against
your lord's life or to drive him, still alive, from his own lands—and in
this land both have been committed. King Edward* was first plotted
against, and then murdered, and after that his body was burned, and
King Ethelred [II] was driven out of his country.† And all across this
land, far too many godparents and godchildren have been butchered,
and all too many holy houses have been destroyed, here and there and
everywhere, because at some earlier time someone had been given
lodging there, and this should not have happened if men knew how
to revere the sanctity of God's peace,‡ and too many Christian people
are constantly being sold into slavery abroad. And anyone who wishes
to will see that this is hateful to God. And how utterly disgraceful it
is to say, and how fearful it is to know, the evil that too often occurs
when men pool their money and together buy themselves a woman,
and all of them commit indecent acts with her, one by one, each after
the other, like dogs indifferent to filth, and then afterwards make
their money back by selling that creature of God—His own purchase,
which He so dearly bought—into the power of God's enemies.

We are also keenly aware of cases where the crime has occurred
of a father selling his child into the power of strangers, for a price,
and a child selling his mother, and one brother selling another, and
anyone who wishes to will understand that these are all great and
terrible deeds. And yet our people are afflicted by things worse
and more varied: there are many among us who break their solemn
oaths, and still more have perjured themselves, and promises are
quite commonly broken. And it is obvious that God's anger bears
heavily on the people of this nation: let anyone understand this who
is capable of understanding.

And alas! how can God's anger bring down greater shame and
disgrace than comes to us on account of our own sins? If a serf should
escape from his lord, and from Christendom, to become one of the

---

*King Edward the Martyr (reigned 975–979). Son of Edgar the Peaceful, he
was assassinated by the followers of his stepmother, Elfrith, mother of Ethelred II.
  †Ethelred II (reigned 978–1016) fled in 1013 but was recalled by the Witan• in
1014.
  ‡That is, the inviolability of religious sanctuary.

pagan• Vikings, and then it afterward happens that lord and serf meet
in battle, if the lord is most foully killed none of his kinsmen will
receive any wergeld•, and if the lord most foully kills the serf he once
owned, then he will pay the wergeld due for the death of a lord. Such
disgraceful laws and shameful taxes have become common among us
because of God's anger: anyone who is capable of understanding will
understand this. And misfortunes fall upon this people commonly
and customarily. And so, this long while, there has been nothing
good, neither at home nor abroad, and all we have known, over and
over again, has been pillaging and hate, and for a long time the En-
glish have had no victories and, on account of God's anger, have
lived in great terror, and the invading seamen have had such power
(with God's consent) that, often, one of them will put to flight ten
of us, and sometimes less, and sometimes more, and all because of
our sins. And often ten or twelve of them, one after the other, will
miserably abuse a nobleman's wife, and sometimes his daughter, or
some kinswoman, while he stands there and watches, he who, before
this happened, had thought himself bold and proud, powerful and
more than good enough. And often a serf ties up, good and tight, the
nobleman who used to be his lord and, because of God's anger, turns
him into a serf. Alas! the misery—alas! the open and public disgrace
that has now come to England, and all because of God's anger! Two
or three seamen will often drive a flock of Christian men from sea
to sea, and throughout this nation, all tied together, to the public
disgrace of us all—if we truly seek to understand anything at all, or
wish to reach any sort of proper understanding. And yet how often,
despite the misery we endure, we repay those who shame us with our
honor and reverence; we continually enrich them, and day after day
they afflict us; they plunder and kill us, they tie us up and insult us,
they steal and rob and carry [us] off in their ships—and lo! what is
so plain and obvious in all of these occurrences but the anger of God
toward this nation?

Nor is it surprising that we fall into such miseries, for we under-
stand perfectly well that, for years and years, men have not concerned
themselves with what either their words or their deeds were accomp-
lishing, but this people—or so it seems—has been exceedingly sinful,
guilty of all manner of sins and misdeeds, guilty of murder and
violence and other crimes, guilty of greed and avarice, guilty of theft

and pillage, guilty of selling men into slavery and the observance of
pagan customs, guilty of treachery and fraud, guilty of violating the
laws of both man and God, guilty of attacking their own kinsmen
and of murder, guilty of breaking the rules of holy orders and of
adultery, guilty of incest and all manner of fornication. And also
guilty, as we have already said, of widespread perjury and oath-
breaking, guilty—far more than should ever happen—of loss and
destruction due to the breaking of pledges and contracts and to all
sorts of lying, and guilty of widespread and frequent profanation of
festivals and violations of holy fasting. Further, this land holds far
too many enemies of God Himself, reprobate apostates and violent
church-haters and fierce, tyrannical oppressors, and this land fairly
overflows with those who despise divine law and Christian conduct,
as well as with hordes of foolish mockers, especially of those things
that most emphatically belong, by right, to the laws of God.

And thus, far and wide, has the wicked custom come to be com-
mon, that men are more likely to be ashamed of good deeds than of
evil ones, because they too often mock at good deeds, and far too
often revile pious folk, and more often than not deride and insult all
those who demonstrate that they love righteousness and have even
the slightest fear of God Almighty. And men act in these ways be-
cause they despise everything they ought to glorify and feel immense
hatred for what they ought to love, and thereby they pervert all too
many others into evil thoughts and evil ways, so that, though they
commit grievous sins and are guilty of constant offense against God
Himself, they feel absolutely no shame—indeed, empty and frivolous
words make them ashamed to make amends for their misdeeds,
as all good books teach. They are like dull-witted fools who, for
weak-willed pride, refuse to save themselves before it is too late and
salvation is no longer possible.

But oh! in the name of God, let us do what we need to do—
let us save ourselves as best we can, so that we do not all perish
together. There was once, in the days of the Britons•, a learned man
named Gildas,* who recorded how, by their misdeeds, the Britons
so provoked God that, finally, He permitted the English armies to

*British historian who died in 570; author of *De excidio et conquestu britanniae*
(The fall and conquest of Britain).

win away their lands and utterly destroy the British nobility. And that happened, just as Gildas said, because the powerful Britons were guilty of robbery, and greed, and avarice, and because there was widespread unlawfulness and perversion of the law, and because of the bishops' laziness and sloth and the wicked cowardice of God's ministers, who all too often stayed silent about the truth and let their jaws mumble when they ought to have been calling out for all to hear. And the people were also guilty of foul extravagance and love of luxury, and of gluttony and every other manner of sin, and therefore their country was destroyed and they themselves perished from the earth. So let us do as we need to, and let such things be a warning to us, for truly, as I have said, we are aware of worse deeds done by the English than anything we have ever heard about the Britons. And thus it is desperately urgent that we take due measure of ourselves and seek most earnestly for the favorable intercession of God. Let us do what we must, bend toward righteousness and at least to some degree begin to give over the doing of evil, and try most devoutly to repair what we have previously broken. And let us love God and observe His laws, and strive most earnestly to do what we (or those who were our sponsors) promised to do when we received the sacrament of baptism. And let us rightly order both our words and our deeds, and most earnestly cleanse our minds, and carefully keep the oaths and promises we make, and maintain some faithfulness among ourselves, without any evil practices. And let us try and try again to comprehend that great Judgment to which we must all come, and try most zealously to protect ourselves against the flaring flames of Hell's torments, and earn for ourselves the glories and the joys which God has readied for those who are willing to do His work on earth. May God help us. Amen.

THE HARROWING OF HELL

"The Harrowing of Hell" ("harrowing" derives from Old English hergian, *"to despoil"), composed in the first half of the eleventh century, is one section of the Latin* Apocryphal Gospel of Nicodemus,* *a third- or fourth-century*

---

*For the source, see J. K. Elliott, *The Apocryphal New Testament* (Oxford: Clarendon Press, 1993), 169–204.

*work that was probably the most influential of the apocryphal New Testament
books. The Old English text falls into two parts, an account of Christ's trial
before Pilate and the Harrowing, which is best known to modern students of
medieval English literature from* Piers Plowman. *This tale of Christ's descent
into Hell to release the souls of the just men and women who had lived before
His Incarnation enjoyed widespread popularity during the Middle Ages. The
Old English version of the trial and the Harrowing exists in two late (eleventh-
and twelfth-century) copies, both incomplete. "The Harrowing of Hell" derives
particular power from its narration in the voices of Carinus and Leuticus, two
men Christ removed from Hell. The Old English version substitutes* seo hell,
*"Hell" (feminine), for the personified Hades of the original; this personifica-
tion recalls the goddess Hel of Norse legend.*

Carinus and Leuticus* wrote as follows, saying:

"Behold! When we with all our forefathers were in the depths of
Hell, a brightness† appeared in that dim darkness, so that we were
all illuminated and gladdened.‡ It appeared suddenly, as if the golden
sun had been lit and was shining above us; and then Satan and all
that cruel host were frightened, and said as follows: 'What is this
light that so suddenly shines down on us?' All the human beings
immediately rejoiced at this immense brightness—our Father Adam
and all the great patriarchs and all the prophets—and said: 'This light
is the Prince of eternal light, sent to us exactly as God promised us
He would.' Then the prophet Isaiah cried out, saying: 'This is Our
Father's light, and is God's own Son, just as I foretold when I was
on earth, as I prophesied and declared that the land of Zebulun and
the land of Naphtali, together with the River Jordan and the people
who sat in darkness, would see a great light, and as I foretold that
those who lived in the kingdom of darkness would receive the light.
And now it has come, and it brings light to us, who have for so long
sat in the darkness of death. So let us all bless and rejoice in this
light.' And then, as they were rejoicing, the prophet Simeon said
to them: 'Glorify Christ the Lord, the Son of God, whom I carried
into the temple in my arms, and what I said was: "You are light and
comfort to all the world, and You are the honor and glory of the en-

---

*Simeon's sons, carried out of Hell by Jesus; they are the narrators, here.

† *Beohrtnys,* here translated "brightness," also means "splendor."

‡ *Geondlythe,* here translated "illuminated," also means "enlightened," and
geblyssigende, here translated "gladdened," also means "blessed."

tire people of Israel." ' And as Simeon said this, all that company of
saints rejoiced exceedingly. And after that there came a sound like the
clap of thunder, and all the saints cried out, saying: "Who are you?"
And a voice answered them, saying: "I am John, prophet of the Most
High, and I have come before Him, so that I may prepare the way for
Him and bring about the salvation of His people."

"And then Adam, hearing this, said to his son, who was named
Seth: 'Tell your children, and these patriarchs, all the things you
heard from the archangel Michael, when I was desperately sick and
sent you to the gate of Paradise, so you might ask the Lord to send
His angel with you and give you oil from the Tree of Mercy, which
[grows] there, so you might rub it on my body.' Seth, Adam's son,
approached the holy patriarchs and the prophets, and said: 'Indeed,
when I was at the gate of Paradise, praying to God, the archangel
Michael appeared to me, and said: "God has sent me to you, for I
am appointed [in charge of] all human bodies. And I say to you,
Seth, that you have no need to trouble yourself with prayers, nor
to pour out your tears, begging for oil from the Tree of Mercy, to
rub it on your father, Adam, for the sake of the pain afflicting his
body, for the five thousand and five hundred years have not yet been
completed, which must come to pass before he will be healed. Then
will come merciful Christ, God's Son, and He will lead your father
into Paradise, and to the Tree of Mercy." ' And when they heard
this—all the patriarchs and the prophets, and all the saints who were
there in that living punishment—they were exceedingly joyful and
glorified God.

"Then it was exceedingly terrible when Satan, prince of Hell and
lord of death, declared to Hell: 'Ready yourself to receive Christ,
who has glorified Himself and is both God's Son and a man. And
even Death is afraid of Him, and my soul is so sick and sorrowful
that I suspect I cannot survive, since He is a mighty opponent, doing
evil to me and also to you; and many that I have brought under
my control—the blind and the lame, the meek and the lepers—He
will take away from you.' Then Hell, terribly fierce and dreadful,
answered Satan, that ancient devil, and said: 'Who is He, so strong
and so mighty, if He is in fact a man, that He is not afraid of Death,
which you and I have long since made our prisoner? Because all those
on earth, over whom you have power, you with your might have

brought down to me, and I hold them fast; and if you are as mighty as once you were, who is this man and Savior that He fears neither Death nor your power? But I know, most certainly, that if in His human form He is so mighty that He fears neither Death nor you, oh then I know that in His divinity He is so mighty that nothing can withstand Him. And I know that, if Death is afraid of Him, He will capture you, and you will suffer eternal misery, to the end of time." Then Satan, prince of the pits of torment, answered Hell, and said: 'Why do you hesitate, and why are you afraid to receive the Savior, who is my enemy and yours? For I tempted Him; and I made all the Jewish people terribly angry at Him, and I excited them to envy; and I arranged that He be pierced with a spear; and I saw to it that He was given vinegar to drink, mixed with gall; and I caused a cross to be prepared for Him, and that He would be hung there, and fastened with nails; and now I am about to bring you His death, and then He will be subject both to me and to you.' And Hell answered, exceedingly angry: 'Be sure you do not let Him take the dead away from me, for many who now dwell within me are anxious to escape. But I know they will not leave me by their own power, unless Almighty God takes them from me, He who took Lazarus from me, though I held him fast, dead, for four nights, but then returned him to life at His command.' Then Satan answered, and said: 'This is indeed He who took Lazarus away from you.' And then Hell said to him: 'Ah! I beg of you that, with all your strength, and with mine, you never agree to let him enter me, because, when I heard that word of command He spoke to me, I was petrified with fear, and all my wicked servants and soldiers were as terrified and afraid as I was, for fear we might not be able to keep hold of Lazarus; but he shook himself, just as an eagle does when he is about to spread his wings and fly off, and that was how he rushed away from us; and the earth, which had held Lazarus's dead body, gave it up again, alive. And now I know that the man who did all this is strong and mighty in God; and if you lead him to me all those locked up in this horrible prison, chained here by their sins, will be torn away from me by His divinity and allowed to live again.'

"But as they were saying these things, there came a voice, a heavenly cry, loud as a clap of thunder, and it said: *Tollite portas, principes, uestras, et eleuamini porte eternales et introibit Rex glorie,* which is, in English, 'You princes,* take away your gates, and raise the eternal gates, so the King of Eternal Glory may enter.' But when Hell heard this, she said to Satan, the prince: 'Leave me at once and go away from my dwelling place; and if you are as mighty as you said you were, before, then fight against the King of Glory, now, and settle it between you.' And then Hell drove Satan from his throne, and said to her wicked servants: 'Lock the cruel iron gates, and throw the iron bolts [into place], and fight against Him with all your might, and hold onto our prisoners, so we are not ourselves taken captive.'

"When the multitude of saints who were there heard this, they cried out in one voice, and said to Hell: 'Open your gates, so the King of Glory may enter.' And then David added: 'Didn't I prophesy to you, when I was alive on earth, "Praise the Lord for His mercy, for He will manifest His wonders to the children of men, and He will smash to pieces the gates of brass and the bars of iron, and He will take them from the path of their unrighteousness"?' And then the prophet Isaiah said to all the saints who were there: 'And didn't I predict to you, when I was alive on earth, that the dead would arise, and many graves would be opened, and that men on earth would rejoice, because salvation would come to them from the Lord?' And, hearing this from the prophet Isaiah, all the saints said to Hell: 'Open your gates; now you will become sick and weak and completely overpowered.'

"And as they were saying this, a great voice, like a clap of thunder, was heard, saying: 'You princes, take away your gates, and raise the eternal gates, so the King of Glory may enter.' But when Hell heard that, called out for the second time, she cried out, once more: 'Who is He, this King of Glory?' Then David answered her, and said: 'I recognize those words, and I, too, sang those words when I was on earth, and I said that God Himself would look down on earth, from high heaven, and would hear the lamentation of His imprisoned servants. And now, you most foul and stinking Hell, open your gates, so the King of Glory may enter.'

"As David was thus speaking, the Glorious King appeared there, in human likeness, He who was our Heavenly Lord, and there was light in that eternal darkness, and He smashed all the chains of sin, and freed all our forefathers from that darkness, in which they

*That is, "princes of darkness."

had dwelled so long. But when Hell, and Death, and their wicked servants, their savage soldiers, saw and heard this, they were terrified, because they saw the incredible brightness of that light, right there in their own kingdom, and all at once they saw Christ sit on the throne, which He had taken for Himself. And they were all shouting and saying: 'You have conquered us! But we ask You: who are You, who without any battle, and without any profanation, but only with Your immense might, have so humbled our power? And who are You, at once so great and so small, so lowly and then so exalted, and so glorious that, in the likeness of a man, You have so overcome us? Ah! Aren't You He who lay dead in the grave and have now come here to us, living, and because of Your death the whole created world, and all the stars, have trembled, and You, out of all those who have died, You alone have been freed from death, You have horribly frightened our entire host? Oh who are You, who have sent that light here and, with Your divine might and shining brightness have blinded the sinful darkness, and at the same time so terrified this entire host of devils?' And then all the devils cried out, in one voice: 'Ah, where do You come from, Savior? So powerful a man and so gleaming in Your might, yet without any stain whatever, and utterly without sin? Until now, the entire world has been subject to us. And most earnestly we beg You: who are You, who so fearlessly have come to us and, in addition to that, will take from us all those whom we have so long held prisoner? Are You perhaps that same Savior about whom our prince, Satan, has spoken, saying that by means of Your death he would come to rule over the whole earth?'

"But then the glorious King, our heavenly Savior, would not allow the devils to go on talking, but trampled devilish Death deep down into the earth, and took hold of Satan and bound him tightly, and handed him over to the power of Hell. And she took him, exactly as our heavenly Lord ordered her to. And then Hell said to Satan: 'Ah, you prince of all ruin and destruction! Ah, you source and beginning of all evil! And ah, you father of all exiles and outlaws! And ah, you who were the lord of Death! And ah, you author of all arrogance! How did you dare plant the idea in the mind of the Jews that they should crucify this Savior, though you knew He was innocent of all sin? And now, because of that tree, and that cross, you have utterly destroyed your happiness; and, by crucifying this Glorious King, you have, most perversely, acted against both yourself and against me—so: understand, now, how many eternal tortures and unending torments you are going to suffer, here in my eternal custody!' But when the King of Glory heard how Hell had spoken to cruel Satan, he said to her: 'Let Satan be in your power, but all the same both of you are damned forever, and, until the end of the world, stay in this place where you have so long imprisoned Adam and all the children of the prophets.'

"And then the Glorious Lord stretched out His right hand, and said: 'All you saints of Mine, you who bear My likeness, come to Me. And you who were brought low and condemned, because of the fruit of that tree* on which I was crucified, see, now, that because of that same tree you will conquer both Death and the Devil.' And all the saints hurried to the Savior's hand, and He took Adam by the right hand, and said to him: 'Peace be with you, Adam, and with all your children.' Then Adam fell and kissed the Savior's knee, and with tearful entreaty, and in a very loud voice, said: 'I praise You, oh heavenly Lord, who wished to free me from this hellish torment.' And the Savior stretched out His hand, and made the sign of the cross over Adam and over all His saints; and then He took Adam by the right hand and drew him out of Hell, and all the saints followed after them. And then the blessed David called out, in a loud voice, saying: 'Sing a new song in the Lord's praise, because God has made miracles manifest to all people, and He has made His salvation known, in the sight of all nations, and revealed His righteousness.' And all the saints answered him, and said: 'Let this be God's glory, and honor to all His saints. Amen. Alleluia.'"

---

*According to the legend, both Noah's ark and Christ's cross were made from the wood of the Tree of Good and Evil.

Social and Instructional Prose

The goals of King Alfred in the late ninth century and of the writers
of the Benedictine Reformation in the tenth century were pedagogi-
cal, aimed at teaching both the Christian religion and the literary
tradition the Anglo-Saxons had inherited from the Romans. The
central concerns of these learned men were the serious decline in
spiritual and intellectual standards of their time and the need to bring
about a state of learning and of faith and works that equaled those of
the Age of Bede. The early eighth-century monk Bede (673–735), the
father of English letters, had written calmly and reasonably about the
history of the English and God's plan for them out of his belief that
knowledge of the great events of the past would enhance the En-
glish people's faith. The concerns of the writers who looked back to
Bede are evident in the translations that follow—perhaps especially
in Aelfric's *Dialogues*. In addition to providing cameo portraits of
various occupations, these conversational exchanges show how Latin
was taught in monastic schools, so that the whole body of Latin lit-
erature, both secular and sacred, might become available to those
already literate in Anglo-Saxon.

BEDE: EXCERPTS FROM THE OLD ENGLISH TRANSLATION OF THE *ECCLESIASTICAL HISTORY OF THE ENGLISH PEOPLE*

The Old English Bede was translated by King Alfred or by scholars working under his direction. The English is less idiomatic than that of Alfred's "Prefaces," and the translator frequently makes tautologous statements (two doublets translating the same Latin word). In Bede's telling, Anglo-Saxon history revealed that God had chosen the Anglo-Saxons to overthrow the sinful Britons•. The Old English translation heightens this perspective, omitting about a quarter of the Latin (principally that with a non-English focus, such as the letters of Gregory the Great to Augustine). The Old English translator concentrates on miraculous events, which Bede himself somewhat downplays.

Two memorable stories in Bede's Ecclesiastical History *are those of the conversion of King Edwin of Northumbria (reigned 617–633) and the first Christian Old English poet, Caedmon (fl. 670). Both emphasize the miraculous, and both show the translator's poetic turn of mind and interest in metaphor. King Edwin hears the appeal of Bishop Paulinus of York (c. 627) to convert to Christianity in the open air, lest the bishop be a magician. Then, in typical Anglo-Saxon monarch fashion, Edwin consults with his council. The pagan• high priest, Coifi, advises him to adopt the new religion. (It is often noted that Coifi's motives are materialistic rather than spiritual—he has not prospered as the priest of the pagan gods.) More moving is the advice of a nameless adviser who compares human life to a sparrow taking shelter from a storm. Thus influenced by his counselors, Edwin becomes a Christian. Bede writes that the sparrow leaves the mead-hall• paruissimo spatio, "in the littlest space of time," but the Old English translator says that he leaves an eagan bryhtm, "in the twinkling of an eye." The Old English expression is both more metaphorical and more memorable.*

The story of Caedmon begins with a dream in which an angel appears to Caedmon and says, "Sing me something." The story has analogues worldwide; the Greek playwright Aeschylus, for example, is said to have been a herdsman when the god Dionysus ordered him to compose tragic drama in his honor.

In the Old English story, Caedmon becomes a monk at Whitby, a "double monastery." The double monastery system began in Gaul and spread to England, Germany, and Spain. It was both a house of monks and a house of nuns under a common administration, normally an abbess. The abbess of Whitby who received Caedmon—and his poetic gift—into the monastery was Hild, who was also abbess during the Synod of Whitby, when the Anglo-

*Saxon church adopted Roman law. The importance of Caedmon's story is
that it memorializes the syncretic impulse that merged Latin and vernacular
cultures, to the profit of both.*

The Conversion of Edwin When the king heard these words[, spoken
by Bishop Paulinus], he answered him, saying that he both wanted
and was bound to accept the faith which the bishop taught, but said,
however, that he needed to consult and take counsel with his friends
and his advisers to see if they would agree, so that they might all of
them together be consecrated in Christ, the fountain of life. Then the
king did as he said he would, and the bishop consented.

Then he spoke to and took counsel with the members of his
Witan•, and asked each of them individually what he thought
and how this new teaching, and the religious worship involved,
seemed to him. And his high priest, whose name was Coifi, answered
him: "Consider, oh king, what this teaching is which has now been
preached to us. Truly, I must acknowledge what I have plainly
learned, that the religion which we have followed, until now, has
no power or usefulness whatever. For there is no one among your
servants who has practiced the worship of our gods more zealously
or willingly than I have, and yet there are many who have received
more gifts and favors from you and have in every respect been more
prosperous. Ah! I am sure that, if our gods had any power at all, they
would clearly have favored me, since I have so earnestly served and
supported them. Accordingly, to me it seems sensible that, should
you find these doctrines newly preached to us better and more
powerful, we should accept them."

Another of the king's principal counselors agreed with these
words, and spoke up, saying: "Oh king, the transitory life we lead
on this earth, in comparison with that time about which we know
nothing, seems to me much like you, in winter time, sitting and
feasting with your noblemen and your warriors, and a fire has been lit
and is warming the hall, while outside it rains and snows and storms,
and a sparrow comes flitting in and flies right through, coming in at
one door and going out through the other. Ah! While he's here inside
the winter storm cannot touch him, but in the twinkling of an eye,
the merest instant, he goes back out into the winter again. Just so is
this life we lead shown to us for only a moment, but what comes be-

fore, and what follows after, we have no idea. Therefore, if this new teaching brings us something more definite and useful, it seems to me worth following." Other ealdormen• and counselors spoke similar words.

But Coifi then added that he was eager to hear Bishop Paulinus say more about the God he preached. And the king commanded that this be done. And when Coifi had heard the bishop's words, he cried out: "I have known for a long time that what we were worshiping was a nothingness, because the more zealously I sought demonstrable truth, the less I found it. But now I freely and openly acknowledge that there shine out from this teaching truths that can give us eternal bliss and salvation. So I now urge you, oh king, that we promptly destroy and burn down to the ground the temples and altars where we have worshiped so fruitlessly."

And lo and behold! The king publicly proclaimed, in the presence of the bishop and everyone else, that he had fully determined to renounce the worship of idols and accept Christ's faith.

And when the king turned to the aforementioned high priest and asked who should profane and throw over the sanctuaries where they had formerly worshiped, the fenced-in temples and altars that were all around them, the high priest answered: "Me, most certainly. Who sooner and more fittingly than I, who have so long and so foolishly worshiped, to now employ the wisdom I have received from the true God, and set an example to other men, by destroying these things with my own hands?" Then, casting away at once the folly of his idol worship, he asked the king to give him weapons and a warhorse—for the high priest was not permitted to carry weapons, nor to ride on anything but a mare—so that he could set about eradicating idolatry. Then the king gave him a sword, and he buckled it on and, taking his spear in hand, leapt onto the king's horse and went straight to the idols. And when the watching people saw him so prepare himself, they thought he had no idea what he was doing, but had gone mad. But as soon as he reached the temple, he hurled his spear, which drove into the wood and stuck fast, and he was exceedingly happy, understanding that he was serving the true God. And then he ordered his companions to tear down the entire temple compound and burn it to the ground.

And the place where the idols used to be can still be seen, not far to the east of York, beyond the River Derwent, and to this day is known as Godmundingham,* where the high priest, inspired by the true God, overthrew and destroyed the altars which he himself had once consecrated.

Caedmon In this abbess's monastery[, at Whitby,] there was a certain brother† who was remarkable for the depth of his religious feeling, as demonstrated by his knack for composing devout and pious poems: whatever spiritual learning he acquired, by listening to learned men speaking, he soon turned into poetic, well-crafted English of the greatest sweetness and inspiration. Indeed, his poems led many men to despise the affairs of the world and to join the pathways of those who pursued the life of Heaven. He was by no means the only poet among the English people, for after him many others began to compose sacred songs, but no one could equal him, because no man, and no human learning, had taught him the poetic craft, for it came to him by divine assistance and as a gift from God. Which was why he could never compose frivolous, empty songs, because he was meant to deal only with spiritual subjects, and his tongue was only suited to the singing of holy songs.

This man had lived a secular life until he was well on in years and had never learned a thing about poetry. And for that reason, when it was time, at the festive table, to celebrate and proclaim the Lord's good tidings, and everyone was required, each in his turn, to sing and play the harp•, as soon as he saw the harp coming anywhere near him he rose from the table in shame and left the feast, and went home to his own house. Once he had done this and left the festive table and gone out to the cattle barn (where he had been assigned to work, that night), and when it came time to rest his limbs he had lain himself down, and slept, until in his dream he saw someone standing beside him, who hailed and greeted him, and spoke to him by name: "Caedmon, sing me something." And he answered, "I don't know how to sing, and that's exactly why I left the feast and came out here, because I can't sing." But the person who was speaking to him replied, "Nevertheless, you will sing for me." And he said, "And what must I sing?" And he was told, "Sing to me about the beginning of things."

---

*Now Goodmanham, near Market Weighton, Yorkshire.
†That is, a monk.

And as soon as he heard this, Caedmon began to sing the praises of
God our Creator, in words and in verses he had never heard before, as
follows:

"Now sing the glory of God, the King
Of Heaven, our Father's power and His perfect
Labor, the world's conception, worked
In miracles as eternity's Lord made
The beginning. First the heavens were formed as a roof
For men, and then the holy Creator,
Eternal Lord and protector of souls,
Shaped our earth, prepared our home,
The almighty Master, our Prince, our God."

Then he woke, and remembered with perfect clarity all that he had
sung in his sleep, and soon added many more words composed in the
same mode, worthily singing of God. And the next morning he went
to the steward who was his overseer and told him of the gift he'd
been given, and the steward immediately took him to the abbess Hild
and repeated what he'd been told. Then she assembled all the men of
the highest learning and their pupils, and when they were all present
she ordered Caedmon to tell them his dream and sing them his song,
so that they might all decide what this was and from where it had
come. And they all said that in their judgment he had been given a
gift by God Himself. And then they recited to him a passage of sacred
learning and directed him, if he could, to turn it into a melodic song.
He agreed to try, and went back to his house, and returned the next
morning and sang them the passage they had taught him in the form
of a most beautiful song.

Then the abbess began to praise and admire God's gift to the man,
and advised and directed him to abandon his secular state and become
a monk, which he was glad to do. And she took him and all his goods
into the monastery, and made him one of that assembly of God's
servants, and ordered them to teach him the entire sequence of sacred
history and all its stories. And everything he was able to learn, from
listening to these accounts, he transformed, after the fashion of a pure
and innocent animal being fed, into the sweetest poems. And his
poetry and singing were so delightful to hear that the very men who
had taught him wrote down what came from his mouth and studied

it. First he sang of the creation of this earth and of humankind, and the whole story of Genesis—that is, the first book of Moses. And afterward [he sang] about the Israelites fleeing from Egypt and coming to the promised land, and many other stories written in the holy canonical Book—and he composed many poems about Christ's incarnation in human form, and then His suffering and passion and His ascension to Heaven, and about the coming of the Holy Ghost and the teaching of the Apostles, and then about the coming of the Day of Judgment, and the frightfulness of Hell's torments, and the delights of the Kingdom of Heaven. And he composed many others, too, about God's goodness and grace, and His judgments on men. In all of his songs he strove most zealously to draw men away from the love of sin and wickedness and to awaken them to love and the dutiful performance of good deeds, because this was an exceedingly devout and religious man, humbly submissive to monastic discipline, and ardently, passionately inspired in his opposition to those who chose to act differently. And for these reasons, when he came to the end of his life he closed and finished it with a good death.

So, as the time of his departure and going forth drew near, he had been for fourteen days mightily oppressed by bodily weakness, but in such a manner that he was always able to speak and walk. There was a sick house nearby, to which it was customary that they took those who were ill and close to death, and there they were cared for. And on the night when he was to leave this world, he asked the man who was taking care of him to prepare a place for him in this sick house, so he might rest there. It surprised the man, hearing this request, for it did not seem that Caedmon's death was so near, but he did as he had been asked to do. And when he had been brought there to rest, he was in an exceedingly happy mood, talking and laughing with the others in that place, and just past midnight he asked whether they had any of the Eucharist•. They replied, saying, "What need is there for the Eucharist? Your departure can't be so near, not when you're talking to us so happily and cheerfully." So he said once more, "Bring me the Eucharist." And when he had it in his hand, he asked whether they were all at peace with him, and if any of them had any complaint against him. And they all answered that none of them had any reason to complain of him, but felt exceedingly friendly. And they asked him if he felt at peace with all of them. And then he answered them, saying, "My brothers, my dearly beloved, I feel exceedingly at peace with you and with all men of God." And he partook of the heavenly Eucharist, which strengthened him, and made him ready to depart for the other life. And still he asked how close it was to the time when the monks would be rising to celebrate God's love and sing their morning prayers. And they answered, "It's not very long." He said, "Fine: we can perfectly well wait until then." And then he crossed himself and laid his head down on the pillow, and soon fell asleep, and thus silently ended his life. And so it had come to pass that, just as he had served God with a pure heart and gentle, serene devotion, so by a serene death he was released from this world and brought to the sight of the Lord. And his tongue, which had composed so many hallowed words, from love of the Lord, thus spoke its last words in His praise, as he crossed himself and commended his spirit to His hands, just before he died. And it is clear, too, from what has been said here, that he had been aware of his impending departure.

KING ALFRED'S PREFACE TO A PRESENTATION COPY OF A TRANSLATION OF SAINT GREGORY THE GREAT'S *CURA PASTORALIS,* PASTORAL CARE

The first work Alfred translated, with the assistance of four scholars, was the Liber Regulae Pastoralis *(Book of the Pastoral Rule), by Pope Saint Gregory the Great, probably in the years 890–896. Gregory was one of the greatest of the early medieval popes, and the English especially venerated him because he had been responsible for their conversion (see the Introduction). The* Cura Pastoralis *describes the ideal prelate; Alfred's preface is a essentially a letter of transmittal, for each diocese, and therefore each bishop in the kingdom was to receive a copy. In the preface, Alfred lays out his educational program. He presents a nostalgic view of the great learning of the eighth century and a gloomy view of an England in which no one south of the River Thames could read Latin.*

Alfred the king greets Waeferth the bishop* with loving and friendly words. And he wishes to inform you how often it comes to my mind that, once, the English people were rich in men both of

*Bishop of Worcester, 873–915.

holy and of worldly learning, and in what blessed times our people
then lived, and how the kings who ruled over the people in those
times were faithful and obedient to God and His earthly messengers,
and how they not only preserved peace and their personal morality
and tranquilly maintained their authority within our borders, but also
extended those borders still further, and how successful they were,
in matters of war as in matters of wisdom, and how eager the men of
God were, in their learning, in their teaching, and in the performance
of all the services they owed to the Almighty, and how men of other
countries came to this land in search of wisdom and learning, and
how we would have to search for them abroad, now, if we needed
them. The decay of learning was so complete, here among our people,
that not many on this side of the River Humber could understand
Mass books written in English, or could manage to translate into
English a letter written in Latin, and I suspect there were not many
who could, on the other side of the Humber; there were so few that
I cannot recall even a single one, south of the River Thames, at the
time when I became king. May God Almighty be thanked that, now,
we have any teachers at all. Accordingly, I direct you, as I believe you
yourself intend, to separate yourself from the affairs of the world, as
much as you possibly can, so that you may pass on the wisdom which
God has granted you. Consider what torments we have suffered, on
this world's account, when we ourselves have neither loved wisdom
nor permitted other men to acquire it; all we loved was to be known
as Christians; not many of us were concerned with putting Christian
virtues into practice.

When I recalled these things, I also remembered how—before
everything was plundered and burned—I had seen churches all across
England filled with books and precious objects, and with great num-
bers of God's servants, who were able to learn exceedingly little from
these books, because they could not understand them, the language
in which they had been written not being their own. It was as if they
had said, "Our ancestors, to whom these buildings used to belong,
loved wisdom and by its means acquired wealth and bequeathed it
to us. We can see their footprints, still, but we cannot follow in their
tracks, because now, being unwilling to bend our minds to trace
that same path, we have lost both the wealth and the wisdom." And,
recalling all this, I was deeply puzzled that all those good and wise

scholars, once so common all across England, who had themselves drawn out all the learning to be found in those books, had never thought to translate them into their own tongue. But then I quickly answered my own question, saying, "It never occurred to them that, later on, men would become so careless and learning so decayed; they deliberately abstained from making such translations, believing that our land would increase in wisdom, the more languages we could command."

And I remembered, too, how the divine law was set out, at first, in Hebrew, and then later, when the Greeks learned it, they translated it all into their language, and all other books as well. And the Romans did exactly the same thing, when they learned it, employing learned interpreters to translate everything into their language. And all other Christian peoples have translated portions of divine law into their languages, as well. And so it seems to me better, if you agree, that we, too, should translate into the language that we all understand those books that we think it needful that all men know, and also, as with God's good grace we certainly can do, if there is peace, that all the sons of freemen now living in England be set to work studying those translations (provided they have the means to do so, and provided that there is no other occupation for which they may be needed), until such time as they have learned how to read English fluently, for thereafter we can teach Latin to those for whom we wish to give further instruction, so that they may proceed into holy orders.

And when I recalled how, earlier, people all over England had lost the knowledge of Latin, though many could still read what was written in English, I began, despite being immersed in all the assorted and many affairs of this kingdom, to translate into English the book entitled, in Latin, *Pastoralis,* and in English, "The Shepherd's Book," sometimes translating literally, word for word, and sometimes according to the meaning rather than the words, exactly as I had been taught by Plegmund, my archbishop, and by Asser, my bishop, and by my priest and pastor, Grimbold, and by my priest and pastor, John.*

---

*Plegmund was a Mercian hermit who was summoned to Alfred's court, was made archbishop of Canterbury in 890, and died in 914. Asser was a monk from Saint David's, Wales, perhaps bishop of Saint David's; he was summoned to Alfred's court in 885, was made bishop of Sherborne about 900, and died in 909. Grimbold was a monk from Flanders who was summoned to Alfred's court in

When I had studied it and was able to clearly understand it, I trans-
lated it into English, and propose to send a copy to each bishopric
in my kingdom, with a bookmark* worth fifty mancus• coins. And
I command, in the name of God, that no man take this bookmark
from the book, nor take the book from the church: there is no way
of knowing how long our bishops—God be thanked—will be such
learned men as there now are all over England, and that is why I want
these books always to remain where they are, unless the bishop him-
self wishes to take it with him, or to loan it elsewhere, or a copy is
being made.

KING ALFRED'S PREFACE TO *BLOSSOM-GATHERINGS FROM SAINT AUGUSTINE*

Blossom-Gatherings *is presumed to be one of Alfred's last translations,
although it survives only in a twelfth-century manuscript and is not attributed
to Alfred by medieval commentators like Alfred's biographer Asser (late ninth
century) and the chronicler William of Malmesbury (died 1142). The work is
a free adaptation of Augustine's* Soliloquies *and bears the influence of works
by Augustine, Gregory's* Dialogues, *and Saint Jerome's Vulgate, his Latin
translation of the Bible. Alfred includes personal anecdotes and speculation in
this work. In the "Preface," he depicts his life's labor, the pursuit of wisdom
and the translation of books. He uses the metaphor of life as a journey in search
of timber, to build both a "transitory dwelling-place along the way" and an
"eternal home." He exhorts his readers to continue their pursuit of wisdom,
echoing the ideas expressed in the "Preface" to the* Pastoral Care.

So† I gathered cudgels and strong staffs, and crossbeams, and
handles for each of the tools I was able to work with, and wood for
building houses, and bent timber for constructing arches, and for
everything I knew how to work with I took the most beautiful trees
I could find to carry off, anywhere in the woods. But I did not bring
home anything that weighed too much, for I did not want to bring

---

893 and died in 903. John was from Saxony; he was later made abbot of Athelney
(c. 880–890).

   *The word *æstel,* translated as "bookmark," may well refer to some sort of
book cover.

   †The manuscript begins abruptly; some text may be lost.

all the wood home with me, even were I able to carry it all. I saw something in every tree that I needed at home. And so I advise anyone who has the ability, and owns a good many wagons, that he travel to the same wood where I cut these crossbeams, and fetch more for himself, and load his wagons with handsome timber, so he can set up many handsome walls, and erect many a rare and splendid house and build many fine towns, and he and his family can dwell there pleasantly and comfortably, whether in winter or in summer, as I myself have not yet been able to do. But he who taught me, to whom this was a most delightful wood indeed, may yet enable me to live more at my ease, both in this transitory dwelling-place along the way, while I remain in this world, and also in that eternal home which He has promised us, by means of Saint Augustine and Saint Gregory and Saint Jerome and many others of the holy fathers. And I believe, further, that as their reward, He will let this way be more accessible than it once was and that, in any event, He will also open my mind's eyes to the light, so that I can search out the right way to that eternal home and to that endless glory, which He has promised us through these holy fathers. May it be so!

Nor is it any wonder that men labor with such timber, both in the carrying of it and in the actual construction, because every man wishes, after building himself a home on land he has leased from his lord (and which his lord has helped him build), that he can now and then rest there for a while, and hunt and fowl and fish, and in all ways possible make use of his leasehold, and provide a living for himself—whether on sea or on land—until he is able to earn his ownership of that land, and his eternal inheritance, by means of his Lord's graciousness and mercy. As the prosperous Giver of Everything will do, He who rules both this transitory existence and that eternal dwelling-place! May He who made both, and who rules both, grant me the power to be useful in both lives, here and especially in that which is to come.

AELFRIC'S *DIALOGUES (COLLOQUIES)*

Aelfric's Dialogues *(also known as* Colloquies*) was written in Latin and follows the classical form of a dialogue between teacher and pupils.*

This translation is based on a colloquial interlinear gloss in one manuscript, presumably written a generation or two after Aelfric's time (Aelfric lived from approximately 955 to 1020). It presents a view of the Anglo-Saxons that is largely missing from the poetry, a glimpse into the lives of such ordinary people as the shepherd, the carpenter, and the smith. Providing an effective contrast between the boldness of the hunter and the timidity of the fisherman, it ends with a lively discussion about which occupation is most essential. The counselor's advice presumably echoes that of Aelfric himself: "Let each be diligent in the practice of his own craft, because he who abandons his craft will be abandoned by that craft."

STUDENT: We young people ask of you, oh teacher, that you show us how to speak [Latin] correctly, for we are ignorant and our speech is sadly imperfect.

TEACHER: What is it you wish to say?

STUDENT: Does it matter what we talk about, if we can say it correctly and profitably, and not either idly or uselessly?

TEACHER: Do you not care, then, whether your instruction involves your being beaten?

STUDENT: We would rather be beaten, and learn, than not learn. But we know you are kind and gentle, and will not beat us unless we compel you to.

TEACHER: And so I ask you: what do you want to talk about? Tell me, if you will, what work you do?

STUDENT: I am a monk in orders, and seven times each day I sing with my brethren, and I am constantly occupied with reading and singing. Nevertheless, when I am not so occupied, I wish to learn how to speak Latin.

TEACHER: What do your fellow monks do?

STUDENT: Some of them are farmers, some shepherds, some oxherds, and others are hunters, and fishermen, while some are fowlers, and some are shoemakers, or salt-workers, or bakers.

TEACHER: And what do you have to say for your-self, farmer? How do you go about your work?

FARMER: Oh my dear master, I work exceedingly hard. I go out at dawn, and drive the oxen into the fields, and then I yoke them to the plow. I don't dare hide at home, even in the harshest winter, for fear of my lord: once the oxen are yoked, and the plowshare has been attached, and the colter-knife• put in place, I have no choice but to plow at least a full acre or more every day.

TEACHER: Do you have anyone with you?

FARMER: I have a boy who uses a stick with an iron point to keep the oxen moving, but right now he has to stay home because of the cold weather, and because he's hoarse from shouting.

TEACHER: What else do you do during the day?

FARMER: To be sure, I do a great deal more. I have to fill the oxen's feed boxes with hay, and I have to water the animals and carry out their dung.

TEACHER: Indeed, indeed! That's a lot of work.

FARMER: Yes, beloved, it's a lot of work, because I'm a serf, not a free man . . . .

TEACHER: Is he one of your brethren?

STUDENT: Yes, he is.

TEACHER: And what do you have to say for your-self, shepherd? Have you any work to do?

SHEPHERD: Yes, beloved, I do. Early in the morning

I drive my sheep to their pasture, and
whether it's hot or cold I stand and watch
over them with my dogs, to keep the
wolves from gobbling them up, and then
I lead them back to their sheepfold, and
twice a day I milk them, and I raise and
lower the bars for them, and make cheese
and butter, and in all things I am faithful
to my lord.

TEACHER: Oh oxherd, and what do you do?

OXHERD: Oh, my master, I do a great deal. When
the farmer unhitches the oxen, I lead
them out to their pasture, and then I
watch over them all night, watching
out for thieves, and later, early in the
morning, I bring them to the farmer,
well fed and well watered.

TEACHER: And is he too one of your brethren?

STUDENT: Yes, he is.

TEACHER: And do *you* have a trade?

HUNTER: I have a trade.

TEACHER: Which is?

HUNTER: I'm a hunter.

TEACHER: For whom?

HUNTER: The king.

TEACHER: And how do you go about your work?

HUNTER: I braid my nets and set them in the right
places, and I teach my dogs to chase after
wild animals, until without knowing it
they come to where I have the nets, so
they get trapped, and once they're in the
nets I kill them.

TEACHER: Can you hunt without nets?

HUNTER: Yes, I can hunt without nets.

TEACHER: How?

HUNTER:	I chase wild animals with my swift-running hounds.
TEACHER:	Which wild animals do you usually catch?
HUNTER:	I catch stags, and boars, and roebucks, and she-goats, and sometimes hares, too.
TEACHER:	Did you hunt today?
HUNTER:	I didn't, because it's Sunday. But yesterday I was out hunting.
TEACHER:	And what did you catch?
HUNTER:	Two stags and a boar.
TEACHER:	How did you catch them?
HUNTER:	I caught the stags in my nets, and I killed the boar.
TEACHER:	How could you be so bold as to stab a wild boar?
HUNTER:	The hounds drove him toward me, and I stood facing him, and stabbed him very quickly.
TEACHER:	You were very brave.
HUNTER:	A hunter can't afford to be timid, because all kinds of wild animals live in the woods.
TEACHER:	What do you do with your catch?
HUNTER:	Whatever I catch goes to the king, because I'm his hunter.
TEACHER:	And what does he give you?
HUNTER:	He clothes me generously and well, and sometimes he rewards me with a horse or a ring, so I'll do my work all the more cheerfully.
TEACHER:	And what trade do *you* follow?
FISHERMAN:	I'm a fisherman.
TEACHER:	And what does your craft bring you?
FISHERMAN:	Food. And clothes. And money.
TEACHER:	How do you catch fish?

FISHERMAN:	I go out in my boat, and cast my nets into the water, and I throw in my fishhook—baited, of course*—and my sieve-basket, and whatever I catch I haul in.
TEACHER:	But what if they're not fish that are fit for eating?
FISHERMAN:	I throw back the ones that aren't any good and keep the good ones.
TEACHER:	Where do you sell your fish?
FISHERMAN:	In town.
TEACHER:	And who buys them?
FISHERMAN:	Townsfolk. I can't catch as many as I could sell.
TEACHER:	What kinds of fish do you catch?
FISHERMAN:	Eels and pike, minnows and cod, trout and lampreys, and whatever small fish happen to be swimming in the water.
TEACHER:	Why don't you fish in the sea?
FISHERMAN:	I do, sometimes, but not often, because I have to do a lot of rowing, when I'm out on the ocean.
TEACHER:	And what do you catch in the sea?
FISHERMAN:	Herring and salmon, dolphin and sturgeon, oysters and crabs, mussels, sea snails, mollusks, flounder and fluke and lobsters, and a lot of others of that sort.
TEACHER:	Would you like to catch a whale?
FISHERMAN:	No.
TEACHER:	Why not?
FISHERMAN:	Because catching whales is dangerous. It's safer for me to go out onto the river with

---

*The words of the original, "*vel* aes," ordinarily mean "whether baited or not." But that reading does not make much sense. The translation assumes, accordingly, that the Old English author (whether Aelfric or someone else) either understood the Latin word *vel* in some different sense or did not fully understand it.

	my boat rather than to join with many other ships and go hunting whales at sea.
TEACHER:	Why is that?
FISHERMAN:	Because I'd rather catch a fish I can kill, instead of one that might not only smash my boat, and those of my comrades, with a single stroke and send them to the bottom of the ocean, but might well kill us all.
TEACHER:	And yet there are many who do catch whales, without endangering themselves, and sell them for very good prices.
FISHERMAN:	You're quite right, but I don't dare try it; I'm too lazy.
TEACHER:	And what do you have to say, fowler? How do you go about trapping birds?
FOWLER:	I catch them in all sorts of ways—sometimes with nets, or with snares, or with bird lime, or by whistling, or with a hawk, or with traps.
TEACHER:	Do you have a hawk?
FOWLER:	I do.
TEACHER:	Can you train such birds?
FOWLER:	Yes, I can. What use would they be to me, unless I could train them?
HUNTER:	Give me a hawk.
FOWLER:	I'll gladly give you one, if you'll give me a swift hound. Which would you like, the bigger one or the smaller?
HUNTER:	Let me have the bigger one.
TEACHER:	How do you feed your hawks?
FOWLER:	In the winter they feed both themselves and me, and in the spring I let them go off into the woods. And then in the autumn, at harvest time, I catch myself some young birds and train them.

TEACHER:	And why do you let the trained ones get away from you?
FOWLER:	Because I don't want to feed them in the summer time: they really eat a lot.
TEACHER:	But many people do feed the trained ones, over the summer, so they can have them ready to hand.
FOWLER:	Yes, they do indeed, but I don't want to do that much work for them, because I know how to get more—and not just one, but lots of them.
TEACHER:	And what do you have to say, merchant?
MERCHANT:	What I say is that I'm truly needed—for the king, and for the ealdormen•, and for the wealthy, and for everyone.
TEACHER:	And why is that?
MERCHANT:	I go off in my boat, and I take my goods and row all over the seas, and then I sell my merchandise, and buy expensive things that aren't made in this country, and then I bring them back to you, over the sea, despite all the many, many dangers, and sometimes I endure shipwreck and the loss of everything I own, barely escaping with my life.
TEACHER:	What sorts of things do you bring us?
MERCHANT:	Silks and purple-colored clothing, precious gems, and gold, strange and unusual cloth, spices and perfumes, wine and oil, ivory and brass, tin and copper and bronze, sulfur and glass, and much more.
TEACHER:	Do you want to sell your goods, here, for just what you bought them for, there?
MERCHANT:	No, not at all. What would I get from all my labor, if I did? Rather, I want to sell at a higher price, here, than what

I bought the goods for, there, so I can earn a profit. And then I'll be able to feed myself, and my wife, and my sons.

TEACHER: You, shoemaker: what sort of useful work do you do for us?

SHOEMAKER: My craft is surely both useful and necessary to you.

TEACHER: Why?

SHOEMAKER: I buy hides and skins, and by means of my skill I turn them into all sorts of shoes and slippers, leggings and leather bottles, reins and harnesses, flasks and all kinds of bottles and other containers, pouches and bags, and none of you could get through a winter without the things I make for you.

TEACHER: Salt-worker, what good does your craft do us?

SALT-WORKER: My craft is tremendously useful to all of you. There isn't one of you who can enjoy a meal, or eating anything at all, unless he makes use of what I produce.

TEACHER: Why?

SALT-WORKER: Is there a man among you who can truly enjoy his food without flavoring it with salt? Who fills his food cellar or his storehouse, except with the help of what I make? In fact, you'd lose all the butter you churn, and all the rennet• you curdle your milk and make cheese with, unless you have my work at hand. You couldn't even keep your vegetables and herbs unless you made use of me.

TEACHER: And what do you have to say, baker? Who benefits from your craft—or would we be unable to live without you?

BAKER:

You might be able to stay alive for a while, without my craft, but not for very long and not very well. Truly, without my craft every table would seem empty, and without bread, eating anything whatever would become deeply unpleasant. I strengthen men's hearts; for men I am the staff of life—and even little children never want to be without me.

TEACHER:

So: what shall we say about the cook? Do we have any need for his craft?

COOK:

If you drove me out of society, you'd have to eat all your vegetables raw, and all your meat raw—indeed, you can't even make a good pot of soup without making use of my craft.

TEACHER:

But we don't really care about your craft, which isn't necessary to us, because we can roast or boil for ourselves whatever needs roasting or boiling.

COOK:

Yes, but if you drive me out, and do all that for yourselves, you'll all be servants, and no one will be anyone's master—and you still won't be able to eat, unless you make use of my craft.

TEACHER:

Ah, monk, you who first addressed me: I've found out that you do indeed have good friends, and very necessary ones. But let me ask you, what are all the rest of them?

STUDENT:

My fellow monks include all sorts of artisans—blacksmiths, goldsmiths, silversmiths, coppersmiths, carpenters, and those who work in many other kinds of crafts.

TEACHER:	But do you have any wise and learned counselors?
STUDENT:	I certainly do. How else could our fellowship be guided and instructed?
TEACHER:	And what do you have to say, oh wise one? Which of all these crafts do you think is the best?
COUNSELOR:	What I say is that God's service is the highest of all these crafts, for as we can read in the Gospel: "First of all, seek out God's kingdom, and His righteousness, and then all other things shall be given to you."*
TEACHER:	But among all the worldly crafts, which is the best?
COUNSELOR:	Tilling the earth, because the farmer feeds us all.
THE SMITH SAYS:	But where then does the farmer get his plowshare, or his colter-knife, if not from my craft? Where does the fisherman get his fishhooks, or the shoemaker his awl•, or the tailor his needle? Doesn't all of it come from my work?
THE COUNSELOR ANSWERS:	Indeed, what you say is true. But we'd all prefer to live with the farmer, smith, than with you. Because he provides us with food and drink. What comes to us from your smithy, except sparks of iron and the noise of beating hammers and puffing bellows?
THE CARPENTER SAYS:	And which of you doesn't make use of my craft—the houses and barrels and boats that I make for all of you?

*Matthew 6:33.

THE SMITH ANSWERS:	Oh, carpenter, why do you say these things, when you know you couldn't make so much as a single hole without my craft?
THE COUNSELOR SAYS:	Ah, my friends, good workmen all! Let us quickly turn away from these arguments, and have peace and harmony among us, and each of us make use of the other's skills—and make sure we are all at peace with the farmer. And let me give this advice to every workman: let each be diligent in the practice of his own craft, because he who abandons his craft will be abandoned by that craft. No matter who or what you are, whether a priest, or a monk, or a peasant, or a soldier, concern yourself with the task before you and perform it, and be what you are, for it is infinitely harmful, and disgraceful, for a man not to know who and what he is and what he needs to be.
TEACHER:	My children, how do you like this sort of talk?
STUDENT:	We like it very much. But you speak very profoundly, and far beyond our ability to understand. Please speak to us so we can understand what you say.
TEACHER:	Let me ask you, then, why you're so anxious to learn?
STUDENT:	Because we don't want to be like foolish animals, for all they understand is grass and water.
TEACHER:	And what is it that you want?
STUDENT:	We want to be wise.
TEACHER:	But in what kind of wisdom? Cunning and crafty, subtle, deceitful, saying good things but thinking wicked ones, speak-

ing soft, meaningless words, but hold-
ing false thoughts in your hearts, like a
whitewashed tomb, all beautiful on the
outside, but with a reeking stench inside?

STUDENT: That is not the wisdom we want, because
he who deceives himself with falseness is
not wise.

TEACHER: What kind of wisdom do you want,
then?

STUDENT: We want to be honest, not hypocrites,
so that we can turn away from evil
and do good. But what you say to us is
too difficult for those as young as we
are. Speak to us as we might speak to
ourselves, and not in such complicated
ways.

TEACHER: I will do precisely what you ask of me.
Tell me, then, young man: what did you
do today?

STUDENT: I did a great many things. Last night,
when I heard the bell ringing, I rose
from my bed and went to the church,
and there I sang night song prayers with
my brethren, and then we sang in praise
of the saints, and early morning songs,
and after that we sang dawn songs, and
seven psalms and the litany and the
day's first Mass. And then we sang the
songs for the third hour of the day, and
celebrated that day's Mass, and after that
we sang the midday service, and then we
ate and drank and slept, and then we got
up again and sang the evening service—
and now here we are, in front of you,
ready to listen to what you tell us.

TEACHER: When will you be singing evensong
or the service that follows the evening
meal?

STUDENT:	When the time comes.
TEACHER:	Have you been beaten, today?
STUDENT:	No, I was not, because I am careful how I behave.
TEACHER:	And your brethren?
STUDENT:	Why should you ask me that? I don't dare tell you our secrets. Everyone knows whether he was beaten or he wasn't.
TEACHER:	What do you eat, in the daytime?
STUDENT:	I still need meat, because I'm young and live my days knowing that I may require to be disciplined.
TEACHER:	What else do you eat?
STUDENT:	Vegetables and eggs, fish and cheese, butter and beans, and all things that are clean and fit to eat I eat with great thankfulness.
TEACHER:	You must be an exceedingly great glutton, if you eat everything that's set in front of you.
STUDENT:	No, I'm not such a glutton that I can eat all different kinds of food at any one meal.
TEACHER:	What then do you do?
STUDENT:	Sometimes I eat one kind of food, and another time a different one, but in moderation, as a monk ought to, and not voraciously, because I'm not a glutton.
TEACHER:	And what do you drink?
STUDENT:	Ale, if I have any; otherwise water, if I have no ale.
TEACHER:	You don't drink wine?
STUDENT:	I don't have enough money to buy myself wine, nor is wine a drink for the young or the foolish but for those who are older and wiser.
TEACHER:	And where do you sleep?

STUDENT: In the sleeping room with my brethren.

TEACHER: Who wakes you up for early morning prayers?

STUDENT: Sometimes I hear the bell and get myself up; sometimes my master wakes me up with a good whack of his stick.

TEACHER: Well, then, young men, you pleasant students, your teacher reminds you to always obey God's commandments and to behave appropriately wherever you may be. When you hear the church bells ringing, proceed into the church in an orderly fashion, and bow humbly in front of the holy altars, and then stand straight, and sing all together, as one, and pray for your sins, and afterward go to the cloisters outside the church, or else go and study.

Medical and Magical Prose

A wide variety of Anglo-Saxon scientific and medical texts is extant. One work is Bald's *Laecboc,* or "Leechbook" (not here translated), a unique manuscript that dates to the mid-tenth century. It includes prescriptions said to have been given to King Alfred by Elias, patriarch of Jerusalem. But the recipes tend to be somewhat repetitive. Medical prose is therefore represented in this book by a selection of charms. These are often labeled "magico-medical" because they blend rational science with ritualistic magic and with prayers and incantations. The charm against warts, for example, uses seven consecrated wafers (seven being the number of completion in Judeo-Christian thought) and ends *amen: fiat,* "amen: let it be done," a formula found in religious texts. The charm to "protect against much walking" includes a prayer in Latin, the most prestigious language of the time. Although the charms have little literary interest, they do provide intriguing insights into Anglo-Saxon ways of thinking.

EIGHT CHARMS

The numbering is the translator's.

  1. In case a man or an animal drink an insect, if the insect is of the

male gender, sing this song (as hereinafter written) in his right ear, and if it is female, sing it in the left ear:

Lonomil odgomil marbumil marbsai ramum toseðtengo docuillo biran cuiðær cærmul scuiht cuillo scuiht cuib duill marbrisamum

Sing this spell in the ear nine times, and say the Paternoster once.

This same incantation can be used against [the bite of] a creeping reptile: sing it into the wound, over and over, and smear it with your spit, and take green centaury herb and beat it into a paste, and lay it on the wound, and bathe it with hot cow's urine.

And if a man should drink snake venom, take mint seed, mix it with wine, and have him drink it.

2. For pain in the heart, take ribwort,* and boil it in milk, and for nine mornings drink it, and you will soon be well.

3. For warts, you must take seven small wafers, of the sort used in making offerings,† and write the following names on each wafer: Maximianus, Malchus, Johannes, Martianus, Dionysius, Constantinus, Seraphion. Then, once again, you must sing the charm (hereinafter set out), first in the left ear, then in the right, and then over the man's head, and then a virgin must go to the man and hang the wafers around his neck,‡ and this must be done for three days, and he will quickly be cured:

A spider-creature came in
with his hands on his hams
and said that you
were his hired horse
lie down on his neck
and so they began
to sail out to sea
and as soon as they'd left
the land behind
they began to cool down
and in came the sister

---

*Plantain, a broad-leaved weed with spiky flowers.
†That is, in saying the Mass.
‡Presumably in some sort of bag.

of a wild animal
and when she was finished
she swore oaths
that this could never
hurt the sick
nor anyone who managed
to get this charm
or anyone who knew
how to recite it!
amen:
*let it be done**

4. For a sudden stitch, [take] feverfew,[†] and the red nettle that grows around men's houses, and broad-leaved way-bread,[‡] and boil them in butter.

5. For lice: a salve: take equal quantities of the herb brimstone-wort, the herb crowfoot, radish, and the artemisia herb known as wormwood, pound them into a powder, knead them together with oil, and spread them over the entire body. Also take the paste made from the brimstone-wort, work it as fine as possible, then dissolve it in hot water, and make the afflicted person drink it. The lice and all the other little worms will soon be dead. Also take equal quantities of wormwood, mint, and myrtle, boil them in wine or sweetened water, and put it on the navel; the lice will all die, and also the other little worms. Also take coriander, boil it thoroughly in ale, and spread it all over the head.

6. If cattle are dying, take groundsel,[§] and the root known as springwort, and the lower portion of cock's-spur grass, and burdock (also known as goose-grass), and put them in hot water, and pour it into the animals' mouths, and they will soon be better.

7. If a man wishes to fight with his enemy, boil bank-swallow birds in wine, and eat them before you fight, and drink spring water afterward.

8. To protect against much walking, to protect against fatigue, take

---

*In Latin, *fiat*.
[†] A chrysanthemumlike plant.
[‡] A plantain or other broad-leaved weed growing near roads ("ways").
[§] An asterlike plant with small yellow flowers.

the artemisia herb known as wormwood in your hand, or else put it in your shoe to prevent fatigue. And just before dawn, pick it up and, before you say anything else,* say: "Tollam te, artemisi, ne lassus sum in via" [Arise, oh artemisia: don't let me be weary along the way]. And make the sign of the cross as you pick it up.

---

*An expansion (but the presumable sense) of *cweþe þas word aerest*, "say this word first."

Glossary

ADVENT The period including the four Sundays before Christmas celebrating the birth of Christ. The word comes from the past participle of Latin *advenire,* "to come to."

ALLITERATION The occurrence of two or more words having the same initial sound on the stem syllable, as in "wily/Words" of *The Husband's Message.* It is sometimes called "initial rhyme."

ATHELING Normally translated "prince," but sometimes "noble." In Wessex, it seems to refer to a member of the royal family who was in line to succeed to the throne because his father had been a ruling king.

AWL A pointed tool for making holes, as in wood or leather.

BOAST A heroic vow; a promise to perform a certain action or die in the attempt.

BRITON An inhabitant of Wales; one of the original inhabitants of the island of Britain before the Anglo-Saxon invasions.

COFFER A strongbox, usually ornamented, holding relics of a dead person.

COLTER-KNIFE A blade at the front of a plow, used for making vertical cuts in the sod.

COMITATUS A Latin term for "train or retinue," borrowed from the Roman historian Tacitus to describe the warband ruled by the *comes,* or "companion"; the analogous Old English terms are *dryht* and *dryhten.*

DOUBLE MONASTERY A system of monastic governance that began in Gaul and spread throughout the Germanic world. It consisted of a house of monks and a house of nuns, under common administration, usually of an abbess. Whitby was a double monastery.

EALDORMAN A nobleman of the highest rank, subordinate only to the king.

ENTAILED (PROPERTY) Inheritable *only* by a specified, unalterable succession of heirs.

ESTATE A noble's dwelling place plus the land associated with it, including the dwellings of serfs and their fields.

EUCHARIST The Christian sacrament commemorating Christ's Last Supper, consisting of partaking of the consecrated elements of bread and wine. It is called "communion" in some denominations.

FOOT A prosodic (metrical) unit consisting of a stressed or unstressed syllable or syllables (see *measure*).

GNOMIC A saying that encapsulates a gnome, a maxim or aphorism that expresses a general truth or fundamental principle.

HALF-LINE Half of a verse line, having two rhythmic stresses and therefore two rhythmic measures, or "feet."

HARP A musical instrument with strings of differing lengths. Old English poetry may have been recited to the accompaniment of a harp or lyre; it is assumed that the music was not so much a melody as a rhythmical beat that enabled the *scop* to keep the rhythm.

HEATHEN See *pagan*.

HEROIC A code of behavior and way of organizing society for war around a lord and his warband that emphasized obedience, loyalty, fortitude, and self-sacrifice in repayment for the lord's generosity.

HOSTAGESHIP During the early Middle Ages, two warring parties who agreed on a peace treaty exchanged noble boys (and sometimes girls). The children were brought up and trained by the foreign king, but they were pledges that their natal family would keep the peace. A dynamic view of hostageship occurs in *The Poem of Walter*.

HYPERMETRIC LINE A line of verse consisting of more than four metrical units—that is, four "feet" or "measures."

KENNING A characterizing periphrasis, always figurative. It is a compound composed of a noun plus genitive complement in which the base-word identifies the referent as something that it is *not*, such as *hildenæddran*, "battle adders," for arrows.

LITOTES A figure of speech in which an affirmative is stated by the negative of its opposite, for example, "This is no small problem."

MANCUS A gold coin worth thirty silver pence.

MEAD An alcoholic beverage made from fermented honey, yeast, malt, and water; modern mead is sometimes made with wine.

MEAD-HALL The central structure of an Anglo-Saxon community, in which rituals of cohesion were enacted, especially gift-giving and drinking from the ceremonial mead-cup, passed from man to man by the lord's wife or daughter.

MEASURE A prosodic (metrical) unit beginning with the stress falling on either a syllable or a "foot" (see *foot*).

NEAR-RHYMES A partial rhyme, either *assonance* (in which the accented vowel sounds correspond but the consonants differ) or *consonance* (in which terminal consonants are similar but vowels in two or more syllables are not).

ORAL-FORMULAIC Poetry composed by an unlettered but traditionally trained oral poet. The formula frames were well established by the time the Anglo-Saxons became literate, so that a literate poet could compose by an analogous (though not identical) formulaic system.

PAGAN An adherent of one of the religions that antedated the introduction of Christianity in the British Isles. The term is also used in *Judith* to describe the Assyrians, the non-Jewish invaders of Israel; it translates the biblical term (in English) *gentile*.

PARALLELISM The use of numerous synonyms, usually listed without conjunctions, in a sentence so that the attributes of a noun are seen to be cumulative. The precise relation of elements is not indicated by subordination, and the elements seem to be parallel.

PERIODIC A sentence composed of hierarchical structures using subordination.

PHALANX Greek term for the order in which ranks of soldiers are drawn up; used also by the Romans.

PICTS One of the ancient peoples of North Britain who were absorbed by the invading Celts between the sixth and ninth centuries A.D.

RENNET A dried extract of the stomach lining of young ruminants used to curdle milk and make cheese.

RING-GIVER An epithet for the king. The king was obligated to reward his followers for their loyal service. This reward often took the form of gold arm rings; hence the king was known as *hringbrytta* (breaker of rings), or "ring-giver."

ROOD A crucifix symbolizing the cross on which Christ was crucified. The Anglo-Saxons and their Celtic neighbors made many monumental stone crosses as well as smaller roods of precious metals and gems.

RUNE One of the letters of an alphabet used by ancient Germanic peoples, especially the Scandinavians and Anglo-Saxons. Each letter represents both a particular word and the initial sound of that word. *Rune* also means "secret writing."

SCOP An Anglo-Saxon English poet who composed poetry in traditional ways.

SOP-CUP A vessel holding liquid (usually wine or ale) in which pieces of bread or other food is dipped or soaked.

SUTTON HOO A royal burial mound at Woodbridge, Suffolk, containing a cenotaph and many grave goods buried in memory of an unidentified king. It was discovered and first excavated in 1939.

THANE A transliteration of Old English *thegn*, an untranslatable category of social status consisting of such people as courtiers, officials, and hereditary and nonhereditary nobles. A *thegn* is always sharply distinguished from a *ceorl*, translated "peasant" in this book.

WERGELD The "man-price"; in Anglo-Saxon and Germanic law, it was the price set on a man's life on the basis of his rank and paid as a compensation by the slayer's family to the kin or lord of the slain man to free the perpetrator of further punishment. The *wergeld* developed into a system of fines graduated according to the extent of the injury as well as the rank of the person injured.

WINTERS The Anglo-Saxons reckoned time by *nights* and *winters*.

WITAN A *wita* was a wise man, counselor, or adviser to the king; the council (or *witan*) was a traditional, loosely shaped, and never wholly defined body. This informal system whereby the king takes his wise men's advice developed into Parliament during the late Middle Ages.

WODEN The chief god of the Proto-Germanic people, often identified with Odin, the supreme deity, creator of the cosmos and humanity, and god of wisdom and the dead of the Scandinavians.

WYRD What happens, or the course of events; fate or destiny (from Old English *weorðan*, "to become"). In Christian times, *wyrd* became identified with the providence of God.

Proposed Solutions to the Riddles

1. Storm on land
2. Storm at sea
3. Storm
7. Swan
8. Songbird (Nightingale? Jay?)
11. Wine
14. Horn
15. Hedgehog
25. Onion (but alluding also to women's sexual pleasure)
26. Holy book; "bird's delight" is a feather quill, used as a pen
28. Ale
29. Moon and sun
32. Ship
33. Iceberg
44. Key (but with double entendre: a penis)
45. Dough (but with double entendre: sexual intercourse)
47. Bookworm
57. Birds (such as swallows, starlings, jackdaws, or crows)
60. Carved rune-stick
66. Creation
87. Bellows